Paranormal
CORNWALL

Paranormal
CORNWALL

STUART ANDREWS
& JASON HIGGS

In memory of Meryl Andrews, 1946-2009

Frontispiece: Granite Celtic crosses, or 'crows' in old Cornish, can be found scattered across Cornwall's awe-inspiring landscape.

First published 2010

The History Press
The Mill, Brimscombe Port
Stroud, Gloucestershire, GL5 2QG
www.thehistorypress.co.uk

British Library Cataloguing in Publication Data.
A catalogue record for this book is available from the British Library.

ISBN 978 0 7524 5261 6

Typesetting and origination by The History Press
Printed in Great Britain

CONTENTS

ACKNOWLEDGEMENTS

There have been many colleagues in the paranormal world, past and present that have helped shape the journey of compiling this book. There are too many to list all of them, but special thanks must go to our colleagues in Supernatural Investigations, for both their company and contributions, including David Hallybone, Clare Buckland and Kevin Hynes, whose enthusiasm and down-to-earth psychic findings are a rare quality. Special thanks go to Francesca and Damian Haydon for developing a more scientific and analytical edge to the group. Also to Becky Andrews, for being so much more than a supportive wife and active researcher, and also for her diligent editing.

Thanks to Dave Wood of PSI (Paranormal Site Investigators) and ASSAP (Association for the Scientific Study of Anomalous Phenomenon) for sharing his thoughts with us.

Also, thank you to Alan Neil and Ron Kirby for their expert dowsing tuition and for sharing some of their secrets and experiences with us. Of course, we could not fail to mention Rita Ratcliffe-Marshall and our friends at Pengersick Education and Historic Trust. In particular the late Angela Evans who, as the castle owner, never failed to welcome us into her home; her passing was a sad event and as a friend she will be sorely missed.

We would also like to thank Murray King Images of St Ives, Cornwall (www. murraykingimages.co.uk) for their help in providing the three illustrations within the Lore of the Sea chapter.

Most importantly, we would like to dedicate this book to our parents, not just for all the childhood memories of a land shrouded in magic and mystery, but for their continued support of what has almost become a way of life.

Every effort has been made to trace copyright holders and to obtain their permission for the use of copyright material. We apologise to anyone who has been inadvertently missed out and will gladly receive any information enabling us to rectify any error or omission in subsequent editions.

INTRODUCTION

Welcome to the county that holds an abundance of history, from invasions to pirates, from myths and legends to mystery and bewilderment – Cornwall has it all! In this book we aim to bring you many unusual stories and experiences from the first, or the last, geographical county in the UK. The Cornish landscape is very special in that it combines large areas of moorland running alongside seaside havens. With its cities and urban areas nestled next to rural towns and villages, all of which sport ancient buildings, it oozes hundreds of years of history.

Derelict engine houses are scattered across moorland, reminding us all of Cornwall's mining heritage. The moors hold other stories of mysterious folk, as well as sightings of big black cats, piskies, crop circles and UFOs. Protruding from the rugged hills, forts and castles can still be seen, with the sounds of battle still ringing out over the strange mists and fog. Seaside towns deceptively hide the many stories of pirates and smuggling, although the coast is still littered with caves and tunnels. Hidden treasure can still be found, buried deep beneath the sea. The coast is awash with old wrecks still waiting to be discovered, lured on to the rocks by bandits to claim their ill-gotten gains. Many people died protecting their ships and treasures from these 'wreckers'.

The authors of this book have had many years of experience investigating and reporting on the paranormal. Being part of an active investigation and research group in south-west England, we endeavour to professionally study and report any unusual phenomena that occurs. We have investigated many locations all over Britain from castles and manor houses to moorland and forests. As the paranormal within Cornwall has been the subject of many previous works, our aim has been to balance revisiting well-documented accounts with venues and cases which are not so well known. Drawing from our own case studies, several of the encounters occurred at venues where we were asked to maintain confidentiality. We apologise to the reader who may be frustrated by not knowing where such events took place; however, we just could not leave out these genuine and fascinating first-hand accounts of the unknown. The majority of places featured within this book are accessible to the general public, so that anyone may have the opportunity to enjoy (or not, as the case may be!) their own experience. We will warmly welcome any accounts from readers forwarded to us via our website, whether they are from a location featured within this book or not.

We hope that you will enjoy the journey you are about to undertake and learn more about the wonderful mystical county that is Cornwall.

Stuart Andrews and Jason Higgs
www.supernaturalinvestigations.org.uk

A good sword and a trusty hand!
A merry heart and true!
King James's men shall understand
What Cornish lads can do!
And have they fixed the where and when?
And shall Trelawny die?
Here's twenty thousand Cornish men
Will know the reason why!
Out spake their Captain brave and bold:
A merry wight was he:
'If London Tower were Michael's hold,
We'd set Trelawny free!
'We'll cross the Tamar, land to land:
The Severn is no stay:
With 'one and all', and hand-in-hand;
And who shall bid us nay?
'And when we come to London Wall,
A pleasant sight to view,
Come forth! Come forth! Ye cowards all:
Here's men as good as you.
'Trelawny he's in keep and hold;
Trelawny he may die:
But here's twenty thousand Cornish bold
Will know the reason why!'

'Song of the Western Men', by R.S. Hawker

Capturing the essence of Cornwall's independent spirit, the song celebrates Jonathan Trelawny, one of the seven bishops confined to the Tower of London in 1688 by James II. He turned away from his Royalist father following the failed rebellion by James, Duke of Monmouth in 1685.

ONE

THE LORE OF THE SEA

Anthony D. Hippisley Coxe writes of Cornwall: 'The duchy is as packed full of beliefs as a can or Cornish Pilchards'; while the *Reader's Digest* describes Britain's folklore as being in a constant state of change due to its turbulent history. Cornwall has seen many invaders, and later visitors, who all leave some of their legends and beliefs behind; inevitably these all intermingle and distort with the passing of years to create a rich tapestry of myths unique to the 'first and last' county in England.

Surrounded by the ocean on three of its sides, Cornwall can be virtually separated from the mainland by the River Tamar, and easily defended. Much of Cornwall's folklore is of Celtic origin, the Celts having been progressively driven into remote areas of the country. Old Cornish as a spoken language had virtually died out by the mid to late eighteenth century, but is of Celtic origin, similar to Welsh and the old Breton tongue. Today it survives only as surnames and place names, such as 'Jynjy' engine house, 'Eglos' church, 'Tre' settlement, 'Pol' lake or pond and 'Pen' meaning hill or headland.

The oceans have always held a sense of mystery to man, with many brave souls perishing at sea or dashed against the rocks. With the sea bringing a lot of the economic activity to Cornwall, a high number of Cornishmen over the years have risked their lives on the water. No wonder, then, that there are so many myths and legends of the sea that have made their way into Cornish folklore. 'From Hartland Light to Padstow Point, is a watery grave by day or night' is one version of the cautionary verse by R.S. Hawker. Off the Isles of Scilly in 1707, Admiral Sir Cloudesley Shovel ran his fleet aground on the feared Gilstone Reef. Two thousand men are said to have died in the raging sea as a result. Some say the tragic loss of life was caused by a sailor who had been hanged for daring to warn the admiral of the impending danger; he had cursed him with his dying breath. The admiral apparently survived this disaster but is said to have had his ring fingers hacked off and then been buried alive by an old woman on St Mary's. While the Isles of Scilly are rumoured to have been home to the most brutal and remorseless wreckers, the far west of Cornwall also had a particularly nasty reputation immortalised in this ancient mariner's verse: 'God save us from the rocks and shelving sands, And save us from Breage and Germoe hands.'

There is a legend of a man who used to ride down on his white horse to Porthgwidden Beach, St Ives for a swim each evening. One night the man did not return from his swim but the horse stayed keeping vigil at the shoreline, initially refusing to move and abandon his master. The horse lived out the rest of his life peacefully but, just after its death, it was seen and heard on several occasions galloping through the streets. The man has also been seen on

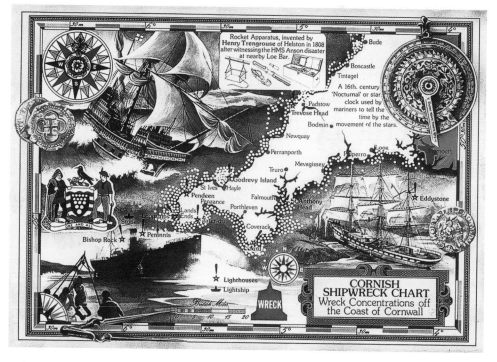

A chart of the concentration of wrecks off the shores of Cornwall, it is believed that as many as 25,000 vessels have come to grief along the Cornish coast.

the shoreline and his footsteps heard in Island Road. Many believe the horse and its master reunited after death and were finally able to make the ride home that they should have made.

Ghostly ships have been seen off St Ives Bay, between St Ives and Hayle, along with ghostly bells heard from deep beneath the waters. There is another sad story of a shipwreck which saw a mother lose her child overboard while being rescued. Day and night she searched the rocks looking for her child; she allegedly died of a broken heart. After her death mysterious lights were seen around the rocks of the bay, and the figure of a woman has been seen, but when approached by concerned passers-by she disappears. There are still reports of both ghosts being seen to the present day.

Croft Pascoe Pool, within Goonhilly Downs, is said to have its own spectral ship, and nearby Kennack Cove and Gunwalloe are said to contain hoards of treasure buried by the buccaneer Avery. Further along the coastline of the Lizard Peninsular is a field known as Pistol Meadow, a sixteenth-century mass grave, following hundreds of deaths after a transport ship went down, shadows of these lost men are reported in the area from time to time. The treacherous nature of the coast along here is further evidenced by a collapsed sea cave, known as 'The Devil's Frying Pan' a 100-metre (unfenced) drop onto the rocks of the sea.

Just west of St Levan is Hella Pointnear, the village of Porthgwarra – once known as Nancy's Garden or Sweetheart's Cove after a farmer's daughter who fell in love with a man who went to sea. This sad tale records how she would keep a constant vigil looking out to sea, eagerly awaiting his return. She had a vivid dream one night that he had been calling to her, so she went out, never to be seen again. Her lover had apparently drowned that same night; it is

Above: *St Ives Bay,
looking towards Hayle
and the direction of where
phantom ships have been
seen. St Ives itself is to the
east (left).*

Right: *Britain's
southernmost point, The
Lizard has seen a great
loss of life along its coast.*

St Michael's Mount has not just been the home of legends, but also of violent struggles between man over the years.

said that both their shades haunt the area to this day. Along the seabed leading beyond this to the Isles of Scilly, and south to Mounts Bay, is the fabled lost land of Lyonesse. Apparently containing 140 churches and many villages, there are numerous reports of people seeing the spires and battlements just poking above the waves. The legend goes that the only survivor of this flood of biblical proportions was a man named Trevelyan, who rode his white horse against the tide. The ancient name for Land's End was 'Pedn' or 'Laaz', meaning end of the earth; there is some evidence to support this with sodden, blackened tree stumps, complete with their roots being visible at particularly low tides in Mounts Bay – another place said to be home to ghostly bells echoing under the waves.

St Michael's Mount takes its name from the archangel Michael who made several appearances here, including one to fishermen in AD 495. Following the Norman Conquest, the Mount was granted to the Benedictine monks of Mont St Michel in 1070, who then built the church at its summit in 1135. A sometimes turbulent history followed, with 6,000 men of Edward IV's Yorkist army laying siege for six months to eighty Lancastrians led by the Earl of Oxford. In 1497 Perkin Walbeck left his wife, for her safety, at the Mount as he launched his own rebellion. In 1549 the Mount was seized by Cornishmen as part of the Prayer Book Rebellion, and in 1588 the first beacon was lit there warning of the Spanish Invasion. The Mount escaped the sacking and burning handed out to so many local towns and ports; believing it to be a fearsome target, the Spanish simply bypassed it. A lucky escape, as there was hardly any powder or shot to man the cannons. The Civil War, which touched so much of Cornwall, saw the Mount besieged for four years. As well as all the bloodshed over the years, the Mount is also home to other legends such as the giant Cormoran, who terrorised the local population before being slain by young Jack the 'Giant Killer'. While in Marazion (derived from 'Marghaisewe' – Thursday's market or market Jew) a ghostly White Lady was said to jump on the back of passing riders and demand to be taken to the Red River near Hayle.

It is widely believed that the Scilly Isles, except St Agnes, had been a single land mass until the Norman period, with the separate islands only taking their current form by Tudor times. Professor Charles Thomas details how, although believed to be separated from mainland Britain for several thousand years, the depth of water between Bryher, Tresco and Samson is so shallow that they are joined at low astronomical tides. A fall of ten metres in the water level would unite all of the Scilly Isles, bar St Agnes and the Western Rocks. Joy Wilson writes of a seventeenth-century Dutch map, showing the seven stones which form the base for the Wolf Rock lighthouse, marked with 'The Gulfe' between them and the mainland. A Latin inscription reveals: 'A land which sank having previously been exposed to the sea.'

Curiously, Wolf Rock is one of the few lighthouses built directly on the seabed. Recent archaeological research further builds on this, as well as the claims of fisherman to have trawled up windows, doors and other debris, by indicating that a dramatic tidal surge did occur, presumably due to seismic activity. The clear line of man-made walls stretches out from the Scilly Isles – Samson in particular – and evidence of submerged huts and burial cairns have been found. An uninhabited island, Samson for many is a peaceful retreat, but others have found the air of timelessness disturbing. Andrew Rothovius suggests that comets could be responsible for the loss of land to the sea, detailing Celtic traditions of the submergence of three large coastal areas in Cornwall, Wales and Brittany; the latter two are the lost land of Cantref Gwaelod, off Cardigan Bay, and the lost city of Ys, which sank beneath the Bay of Douarnenez. With global warming causing a rise in sea levels, combined with the danger of earthquakes and natural disasters, how much of Cornwall and indeed, Britain, will be left in a thousand years time?

Sennen Cove was not just the scene of many wrecks and deaths associated with smuggling, it was also the home to a most unusual guardian spirit. Known as the Hooper, it was a mist-like

Sennen Cove boasts a most spectacular beach, but is also said to be home to mysterious sprits and murdered souls.

cloud which settled on Cowloe Rock hooting to fisherman not to sail by day and emitting a shower of sparks by night. The legend continues that one day a fisherman and his son beat their way through the cloud, and neither they nor the Hooper were ever seen again.

Some 300 years ago, a smuggler named Ralph Penrose took to the sea with his infant son following the death of his wife. On their return they were wrecked off Cowloe Rock, with Ralph's brother, John (who had been left to care for the estate) watching and making no effort to help. The boy, rightful heir to the Penrose legacy, survived but was murdered on his uncle's instructions. Their cousin William also survived, but lost his memory and was only able to expose John after hearing a disembodied voice revealing the crime. John later hanged himself, but William could find no peace at Penrose due to the spirits haunting the manor.

Three of the Supernatural Investigations team were fortunate enough to have taken part in a study here during May 2005. Penrose is an almost isolated, by modern standards, manor used as a farmhouse on the Land's End peninsular. There is a most spectacular and highly colourful plaster relief, dated 1668, above the fireplace displaying two crests either side of a triangle, with an eye surrounded by a circle within. This symbol of a 'Third Eye' certainly did lend a mystical feel to the building, but the majority of the house had a calm and homely feel. Upstairs, the Apple Room feels a lot colder, and is one many people have refused to sleep in due to the oppressive feel. The Shirley Room really did have an uneasy, heavy atmosphere and, after encountering an isolated cold spot which came and went, all of the team said they would refuse to sleep in here. Along the corridor a spectral figure was witnessed by an experienced investigator who, quite out of character, had to leave early. It was entirely confirmed that no

The plundering of ships was a dangerous occupation, as those caught could face execution; their opponents, the revenue men, also frequently risked injury or death at the hands of disgruntled looters.

Mythical Tintagel, one of Cornwall's most beautiful shorelines and one that many find charged with a special energy.

one was in that area at the time. Within the floor of the barn is a most unusual stone carving of three circles, which looks to be of ancient origin; who put it there or why is still an unsolved mystery.

Whether deliberately lured onto the rocks or not, a wreck would often see the poorest descending onto the beaches, stripping all timber from the ship, along with any valuables and clothing from survivors. One can only feel sorry for the poor sailors who survived to encounter such a drunken riot – which would often claim their lives as well as all possessions and clothes. Wrecking and smuggling were far more profitable pursuits than mining or fishing; many accounts estimate more spirits were being smuggled in through Cornwall and Devon by 'Free Traders' than legitimately through London's docks. John Carter from Breage, also known as the 'King of Prussia', was one of the most notorious, his base at Prussia Cove being surrounded by a ring of cannon. Sinking revenue cutters and robbing Penzance's customs house were a few of his fabled crimes.

A figure has been seen in the window of Dead Man's Hut – a small stone building originally perched half-way up the cliffs, serving as part of the defences and lookout for Portreath. It was also used as a temporary mortuary for any poor wretch washed up on the beach. Nearby is Smugglers Cottage, now a private house; there is a cave which is still partly accessible and it is rumoured that tunnels lead from here back to the cottage and were used by the smugglers. While the building was being renovated a secret room was uncovered, along with an old sea chest, cutlass and the skeleton of a man sat in a chair. The building has previously been used as a guest house, where a figure of a man in his twenties, dressed in Jacobean clothing, has been reported by disturbed guests.

Tintagel is, according to one version of the legend of King Arthur, the birthplace of the fabled king. Uther Pendragon, then King of Britain, seduced Ygraine, the wife of Gorlois, Duke

Standing at the edge of Merlin's Cave, looking across at Barras Nose, which is said to have a special atmosphere – and a collection of spectral monks.

of Cornwall, aided by the sorcerer Merlin. Uther disguised himself as the duke and deceived his way into her bed-chamber. It was said that from this illegitimate coupling Arthur was born.

The views from the head are truly awe-inspiring, and if ever there was a place from which a legend could begin, then this is it. The castle ruins that occupy this dramatic point of the Cornish coastline are actually from a much later date than that of Arthur. However, one cannot disregard the fact that the ruins have provoked tales of an age long gone or ignore that the ghost of Arthur himself is said to wander here. The sheer majesty of the Atlantic Ocean, as it beats mercilessly against the stony cliff face, conjures up powerful images of knights, majestic battles, sorcery and mystery.

Another frequently recalled version states that the infant Arthur was delivered from the sea to the awaiting Merlin, who had cheated the Devil and his plan to create a satanic child. It was here that the infant king began his first few days inside the cave at the foot of Tintagel Head, sheltered by Merlin. Known as Merlin's Cave, it lies on the small beach that spans between Tintagel Head and Barras Nose. Only accessible with the correct tide, Merlin's Cave overflows with atmosphere, making it all too easy to picture a wizard casting ancient magic over a newborn king. Camleford also has 'Arthurian connections', being linked with the mystical Camelot, as does the gruesomely named Slaughter Bridge, which is believed by many to be the site of the Battle of Camlan. This battle saw Mordred fatally wound the king, who was borne away on a barge accompanied by his black maidens to Lyonesse. Historically opinion on this is divided, as with any Arthurian legend or site, but there must have been some brutal battle to explain the name and the shadows witnessed from time to time making their way across the bridge.

Not far from Tintagel is Blackways Cove, close to the beach of Trebarwith Strand, rumoured to be haunted by the spirits of dead sailors congregating after being washed along the north Cornish shoreline. In Polperro, Willy Willcock's Hole is said to be home to this unfortunate fisherman's cries, as his spirit continues to try and escape the labyrinth of tunnels within.

TWO

MYSTERIOUS MANORS

As it would be impossible within this book to detail all the Cornish halls and manors with spine-chilling tales associated with them, the following is an account of some of the ones we have investigated, along with a few of our favourite tales. Others include Kenegie House, Penzance, which is home to phantom laughter and voices along with a woman in black floating through the corridors; Port Eliot Manor House, St Germans, which saw a party abruptly end during the 1980s with the appearance of a spectral monk witnessed by several guests; and Antony House near Torpoint, which was said to have been home to what could be termed a 'crisis apparition' during 1880. It was here that a maid caring for Helen Alexandra was shocked to see another woman enter the room and, after standing by the bed, subsequently disappear.

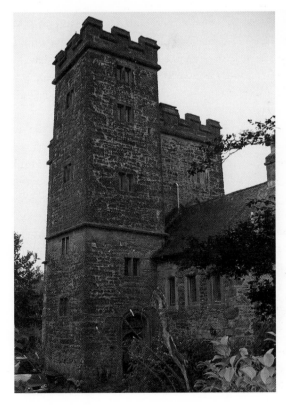

A few hours later Helen slipped from this world; when her mother visited from Scotland, the maid recognised her as the spectral visitor, despite never having seen her or her picture before.

Castle Horneck Manor, Alverton, Penzance

Some of the reported ghosts here include a phantom coach and horses, along with the spectre of a man along the driveway. Several of the team have had the pleasure of working alongside the practising dowser, Ron Kirby, here. Ron describes the site and its previous guises as 'A mismatch of periods: Iron Age, Medieval, Elizabethan (until it was burnt down by the Spaniards in their

One of Supernatural Investigations' ongoing case studies is the enigmatic Pengersick Castle.

The Georgian interior of Castle Horneck, featuring a picture of nearby St Michael's Mount.

attack on Penzance in the late 1500s). It was later rebuilt as a Georgian building and is now used as a youth hostel.'

The castle title is presumably derived from the former twelfth-century 'Iron Castle', said to have been built here by the Tyes family – apparently aptly named due to its formidable defences. Having made at least three visits between the team, we have largely found the ground and upper levels to be calm, and have sadly not encountered the 'White Lady Margaret', said to loiter by her portrait on the grand staircase. In contrast, the basement level has a most unusual feel to it, the laundry in particular having a very heavy atmosphere. The dining room, kitchen and games room also give off strange feelings and are home to encounters with the unknown, including a muffled laugh being heard in the games room. The internal stone wall in here is very strange

and appears to be relatively new in comparison to the rest of the building. Perhaps there is some truth in the rumour that there is another room behind. Compounding the secret passage myth is the fact that the original flagstone floor in here has a peculiar hollow sounding area. Misty figures and inexplicable bangs and crashes from the kitchen have all been experienced, including one occasion when the noises were heard by several people and recorded on a camcorder. It was clear that these sounds originated from within the room, and that no one had entered, but, somewhat bizarrely, there were no visible signs of anything moving.

Castle Horneck's grand staircase, said to be the haunt of a White Lady.

Cotehele, Calstock

Set above Halton Quay on the River Tamar sits a gorgeous and mysterious looking manor, set back in acres of woodland. This medieval house was altered during Tudor times and was the ancestral home of the Edgcumbe family when William Edgcumbe married Hilaria de Cotehele in 1353. The name Cotehele is derived from the Cornish 'Koesheyl' loosely meaning 'the stream in the wood'. Cotehele was owned by the Edgcumbes for nearly six centuries until the National Trust eventually took possession of the manor house in 1947. The present house was built between 1485 and 1539 during the reigns of Richard III, Henry VII and Henry VIII. Sir Richard Edgcumbe, who was rewarded for his loyalty to Henry Tudor at the Battle of Bosworth (1485), started to completely remodel the original thirteenth-century property with defence in mind. A lot of the exterior windows are positioned high up and are very small in size.

At the time of Richard Edgcumbe the house looked smaller, with various areas of virgin land surrounding the location; this was soon to be built on. It was at this time that Richard became a vigilante, believing the king was responsible for murdering the princes in the tower – though this was never proven. He took refuge at Cotehele, and its many acres of land, attempting to escape the rage of King Richard III and his entourage. Today, a small chapel denotes the location in the woods where Richard managed to conceal himself from the king's agent, Henry Trenowth. Henry Whitfield cleverly summed up the forward thinking that saved Richard's life in the following excerpt:

> Vainly they raised the ornate tapestries to see that no culprit was concealed, irreverently they trespassed the aisle of the chapel, as through its 'panes of storied glass scarce could the light of morning pass' and they ransacked the hall, so that no knight should breathe under headpiece or skull cap, corselet or armour. Realising that Edgecombe had gained the woods, the pursuers raised the hue and cry, and the sorely pressed fugitive placed a stone in his cap and threw it in the river. The stratagem was successful, and Bodrugen's retainers were ruefully contemplating the eddy caused by the splash as Edgecombe penetrated the recesses of a secret cave.

The earliest report of spooky occurrences relates back to 1742, when one of the many Edgcumbe ladies was laid to rest in the chapel at Cotehele. The night after the funeral a knavish sexton made his way down to the chapel, opened the vault where the body was kept and then forced open the coffin. There, as the woman lay in full regalia and jewellery, he attempted to prise the priceless rings from her lifeless fingers. At this point the corpse began to stir and she opened her eyes and looked straight at the thief. You can imagine his dismay as he dropped everything and ran for his life. The lady, who had been in a coma and was not dead, got out of the coffin and made her way back up to the manor, using the lantern the thief had so kindly left behind.

Supernatural Investigations investigated this amazing location in early 2009 and the team came away with some interesting anomalies caught on camera and audio digital recorder. One such picture was taken in the Great Hall with a 10mp Panasonic Lumix TZ5 digital camera. The shot was set up to encompass the entrance to the Great Hall from the corridor and included one of the team members clearly displayed to the left of the photo. The camera was placed on a table as the picture was taken. At first the anomaly was not recognised and was not noticed until later into the investigation. At this point, the same two team members went back into the Great Hall and recreated the exact same scenario in an attempt to explain the phenomena. However, after twenty minutes of re-enactment, the same picture could not be recreated. In the first picture there was a shadow of what seemed to be a figure by the entrance, in the second picture this was not the case. The shadow seemed to be of someone with their hands on their hips, yet there was no physical figure anywhere near. This photo has been seen by many different people, none of whom can explain how the shadow would have been cast, based on the trajectory of the light and the lack of a physical being to cast from.

Other evidence reportedly captured by previous investigation groups includes video evidence of what appears to be three separate orbs floating above the stairs between the Punch Room and the White Room. They seemed to vary in size and floated independently of each other, although seemed to be acting intelligently. This piece of evidence has stirred questions in the most sceptical of people, including the House and Collections Manager, Rachel Hunt, who said 'There must be a scientific explanation, but it remains the most convincing paranormal event I have witnessed in my seven years at Cotehele.' Rachel admits that she is normally sceptical, having worked at Cotehele for many years, but seems at a loss to explain this intriguing footage.

The manor house seems to have many spooky inhabitants, but one occupant is seen more frequently than others. She is famously known as the 'White Lady' or the 'Lady in White' and is often witnessed descending the main staircase along with ghostly music heard throughout the house. She has also been seen in certain bedrooms and on one occasion was possibly seen by a previous live-in nurse to Mrs Julyan. She claimed to have seen who she thought was Mrs Julyan's daughter, only to be told by Mrs Julyan herself that she lived at Cotehele Manor alone. Did she see a full manifestation of the 'Lady in White'? The nurse's account was also witnessed by an electrician working at the manor, who had his own experience with an entity when he was just an apprentice. While he was working alone he could hear what seemed to be footsteps on the floor below him. As the sound dissipated the contractor suddenly felt an 'icy chill' move through him. Immediately afterwards, the door at the end of the corridor slammed and then rattled. It was enough of an experience to leave him 'shaken and terrified'.

Cotehele house is a popular attraction for schools of children learning about history. Thousands of children have probably ambled along the historic floors of this amazing manor, bringing their own energies and creating their own positive atmosphere. It is not often that paranormal experiences have been reported by children, although some have recounted their feeling of being watched or generally feeling uncomfortable. On one occasion it was reported that a particular child may have seen a manifestation of more than one spirit. While on a school trip this child asked why there was a line of school children against the wall in the next room. On investigation, it was revealed that the room was empty and no children had occupied it.

There are many, many more accounts of personal experiences and alleged scientific evidence to support the theory that Cotehele is haunted. A definite place to visit if you can!

Trevarno, Crowntown, near Helston

An official world heritage site, Trevarno is now famous for its extensive gardens and organic skincare products, but was previously connected with the Cornish mining industry. Members of the SI team took part in an investigation here during 2005. You can find out what we

The entrance to Trevarno House. Its main historical claim to fame is from the 1874 -1994 owners, the Bickford-Smith family, who invented the miners' safety fuse.

Trevarno's 700 acres of landscaped gardens and woodland, rumoured to have their own stories to tell, as parts date back to 1246.

encountered at www.supernaturalinvestigations.org.uk/investigations. Visitors to the site may be pleased to know that the majority of unusual encounters took place within the offices. The middle office in particular had an eerie and uncomfortable feeling to it, while the sounds and sensations of someone quickly moving past you were experienced by several of the team in one of the other offices and the corridors. What could be termed as poltergeist activity was also experienced, with a set of dowsing rods placed on a work surface heard to move on their own accord. At one point, a hotplate in the kitchen turned on of its own accord; several investigators present were able to verify that no one had gone near it, and the staff who accompanied us were deeply concerned as it had never happened before and has no timer function.

Trerice, near Newquay

This is the former home to the Arundell family, notably the fifth Sir John Arundell. He had been the governor of Pendennis Castle, Falmouth during the Parliamentarian siege of 1646. After the neighbouring St Mawes Castle surrendered without a shot being fired on 12 March, Arundell held out until 15 August when he could no longer watch the men and women inside starve and succumb to illness.

Numerous visitors to this grand house have reported a feeling of standing still or travelling back in time as they explore its many rooms. A First World War era guidebook to Newquay describes Trerice as 'An ancient baronial mansion which the country people still declare to be haunted by the unhoused spirit of a certain passionate Lord of Arundell, known in the neighbouring villages as "the wicked lord".'

During renovations in the 1980s, workmen in the north wing reported the sense of a presence, a swishing sound and doors opening of their own accord. This has also been experienced by staff and visitors, and more commonly the smell of lilac perfume which accompanies the feeling of an invisible, or at best shadowy, figure of a Grey Lady, seen gliding along the north wing and down a long-removed spiral staircase. The legend is that this was a servant girl, seduced by the 'wicked lord', who subsequently committed suicide. Also said to appear in the courtyard is the ghost of a poor stable boy who was trampled to death by the horses in his charge. Since the 1980s the accounts of encounters have diminished; perhaps since completion of the works at the house, the phantoms of Trerice have finally found peace?

Penfound Manor, near Bude

Just outside the village of Poundstock (derived from 'cattle pen' or 'pound') is the ancient Penfound Manor. The site was originally a Saxon settlement, then occupied by the Normans before the Penfound family took residence in the twelfth century. Recorded within the Domesday Book, this private residence has seen alterations from the Tudor and Stuart periods and is said to be the oldest inhabited manor house in England. It also boasts the only working example of a fourteenth-century Guildhouse, and a collection of former residents that include a friendly ghost – although details are scarce. The well-known story is that of a trio of spirits who return on the anniversary of a Civil War tragedy. Kate Penfound attempted to elope with her lover and neighbour, John, of nearby Trebarfoot Manor. Kate's father, Arthur, was a staunch Royalist, so on discovering his daughter attempting to flee with a Parliamentarian supporter, he is said to have drawn his sword (or pistol) and all three died as a result. Their ghosts are said to walk the manor and re-enact their tragic skirmish on 26 April each year. A woman presumed to be Kate has been seen peering through her bedroom window, looking out for her lover to appear to carry her off. Murmured voices, along with bangs and crashes, have also been heard coming from within the empty room.

Nearby in St Neot Church the spectre of Revd William Penfound is also said to re-appear kneeling at the altar, as he would have done celebrating mass in December 1356, when he was charged upon and murdered by unknown assailants. John Beville and Simon de St Gennys were charged with his murder, but not convicted and so the murder remained unsolved; some say the spirit of the priest returns, dissatisfied that justice was never carried out.

Lanhydrock House, near Bodmin

During November 2004 a few of us were part of an investigative team called in by the National Trust to try and add substance to the stories and experiences reported by staff and visitors.

The majority of the house is strikingly quiet, especially the billiard room which seemed to almost make time stand still. Within the smoking room, it was suddenly noticed that a curtain cord was swinging of its own accord. The window was past the roped-off desk, so could not have been caused by any of the team. It appeared to pick up pace, before settling at a constant swing for the rest of the session, even after we had stopped it. It continued knocking against the window sill loud enough for all to hear. Unfortunately, we did not encounter the smell of phantom cigar smoke that has been reported in here.

While in the kitchen, the heavy chain on the giant roasting spit

The woods near Lanhydrock, said to contain the soul of at least one man hanged during the English Civil War.

also appeared to be swinging freely, although it could not be confirmed that someone had not leaned or brushed against it. The nursery and the corner of the middle room in particular had a very strange and unwelcoming feel, although this was arguably a natural reaction to the collection of antique dolls and the formal, but creepy, atmosphere. Within the gallery – a vast open space with a magnificently sculptured biblical relief ceiling – an inexplicably sad feeling was reported by many. Just prior to this, one of the team felt a sharp pain on her neck accompanied by a slight burning sensation; on inspection, three small scratches had appeared on her neck. Perhaps the Grey Lady of Lanhydrock, presumed by many to be Isabella Robartes, chose not to show herself but to make herself known by other means? There is another, later, Lady Robartes reputed to haunt here, who was rescued from upstairs during the fire of 1881 which consumed the house. Could this strange scratching be a replay of one of her injuries as she climbed out of the window to later die of shock?

As a footnote, our colleague Dave Hallybone recalls his own strange experience from Lanhydrock during the spring of 2004.

> The house was relatively quiet due to the time of year and we were walking from room to room with very few people in the vicinity. When we got to the playroom we were looking at the many toys, including a rocking horse and a large dolls' house behind the velvet rope. As I turned around to look at the other side of the room I felt a strong tug on the back of my trousers. Thinking that I had bumped into the velvet rope, I turned around to see that I was about 3ft away. My wife then asked me what I was looking for, so I explained what had just happened, and she joked that the ghosts were pulling my leg. As we looked into the first bedroom on the left, for no apparent reason the motion sensor went off. Luckily for us there was a member of staff who could see we had not tried to enter the room. We proceeded up the corridor towards her, and a second sensor went off; we did not stop and headed towards the end of the corridor as a third chime began. Asking about the sensors and if they go off on their own often, she replied they did not, which left us both nervously walking away, wondering if a ghostly child had just been playing a game with us.

Prideaux Place, near Padstow

Completed in 1592, the ancestral home of the Prideaux-Brune family is said to be haunted by at least two ghosts, both seen on the staircase: a lady in a grey dress, along with a pretty unique lady in green, who has also appeared in other rooms of this vastly extended gothic masterpiece. Her sudden appearance has startled several staff and contractors, causing at least one of them to literally run from the property in fear. There are also rumours of a spectral growling dog being encountered at the foot of the bed in one of the many rooms, and a small child seen running into the pantry, never to emerge. The house has also been featured on the big screen, having been used for the setting of the hunt scene in *Omen III* starring Sam Neill.

Bodilly Manor, Wendron

In 1730 a fire destroyed most of the original house which dated from the 1400s, the current manor being a single grand farmhouse which was originally two cottages, now connected together. Wendron was a district heavily mined for tin and the remains of several ivy-clad engine houses can still be seen today. Nearby Poldark Mine remains open as a tourist attraction, but there is a multitude of other long since capped tunnels and passageways running under the ground. Mining was a particularly dangerous occupation, and the source of many superstitions such as 'knockers and tinners' (*see* chapter 6). So it is not surprising that from this, and the practice of smuggling, that under the grounds of Bodilly is purported to be a secret passage believed by many to contain a hoard of treasure.

The current owner, Jonathan Hodgetts, describes how the first six months or so in his new home were quite uneventful. It was only once renovations commenced – including the removal of fireplaces – that sightings, the feeling of being watched and, on one occasion, a bedroom doorknob rattling and turning on its own began. The smell of burning wood was experienced along with phantom voices being heard from downstairs. In his own words, 'As to activity here – there is always something going on in one way or another.' Although, he does state that unfortunately he has never discovered the secret tunnel, said to be home to the legendary treasure.

The Ghost Club Society, amongst others, have visited and investigated Bodilly Manor; their findings include a group witnessing a heavy wooden table shake and seemingly begin to rise of its own accord. Our colleague, Kevin Hynes, took part in one such vigil during 2005 and he recalls how a wealth of information was gained through psychic methods by the team, and that while in the kitchen he felt a most unusual cold breeze, isolated to just his right hand, while sat at the same heavy table. One possible reason for the haunting comes from a terrible mining accident in 1858 when a group of seven miners were trapped following an explosion; suffering a terrible death by suffocation, sadly their bodies were never recovered.

Bodilly Manor.
(Photograph kindly
provided by the owner)

THREE

POLTERGEISTS

The word poltergeist is German, from *poltern*, meaning to make a rumble or noise and *Geist*, meaning ghost or spirit. Although poltergeist stories date back to the first century, the evidence supporting the existence of poltergeists is anecdotal, which is hardly surprising as the nature of the phenomenon is unpredictable and sporadic.

There are reportedly five steps to poltergeist activity, starting with the senses of the body. Typically, you might see something out of the corner of your eye or hear footsteps; you may feel cold spots or whiffs of discernible smells. The next stage is communication – hearing whispers or moans when alone, a quick breeze moving past you when all doors and windows are shut, or unusual marks appearing on the floors or walls. The third stage is the physical aspect of the haunting. Lights may turn on and off on their own, you may feel like you've been touched or pushed, furniture may shake or move, objects may appear to jump off units, objects could disappear and then turn up elsewhere, dark or light shadows might appear and unusual markings may show on the skin as if from slapping or scratching. The forth stage is where the entity learns about you, finding your strengths and weaknesses so that it can inflict the most terror. It attempts to play tricks on you by exploiting your utmost fear. Finally, the fifth stage is the most dangerous: the energy produced can seriously inflict harm and move larger objects. It may fully manifest and at this point can begin the whole process again.

Bodmin Jail. Many people have reported poltergeist phenomena here, but is it the building or their own influence?

Usually, following the fifth stage there is a dormant period where the poltergeist attempts to regain its energy and starts again from the beginning. It should be noted that this type of poltergeist activity is extremely rare and is the worst case scenario. In most cases people will only ever experience the first two stages – which do not necessarily constitute a poltergeist, but simply a haunting.

While you may think that this sort of activity will occur in well-known haunted locations, the truth is that it is usually associated with people in their homes. Poltergeist activity tends to be linked to people and not locations and therefore when people move, so do the poltergeists. There seems to be a high correlation between poltergeist activity and homes with teenagers and it appears that the pubescent stage can create a lot of energy for manifestations to utilise and build on. Due to the way this unusual phenomena is experienced a lot of cases go unreported or unnoticed, with people choosing to cope with the frightful encounter alone. Most people do not want to be associated with the stigma that follows such an account and the type of press they would receive.

In May 2005, members of Supernatural Investigations were called to three private houses in Liskeard after reports of activity including moving objects and light bulbs blowing simultaneously. Ron Kirby, a professional dowser from Cornwall, had visited the properties on numerous occasions before the investigation to perform a 'soul rescue' which involves leading the malevolent spirit 'into the light'. Even though this had calmed the situation, paranormal activity was still occurring. During the investigation many strange events occurred, but most notably we had an incident involving a flying toy. As the investigators moved from a little girl's bedroom onto the landing they heard a noise as if something had been thrown. When they switched on the lights, and looked down, it was apparent that a toy had 'followed' them out of the room; the room at this point was empty, with all the investigators standing on the landing. When the little girl was questioned as to where the toy had been located in her room it was obvious that it had travelled some distance, seemingly on its own.

According to the Paranormal Database online, other varieties of Poltergeist activity include a spirit named 'Plucker' who haunts the Napoleon Inn at Boscastle. This poltergeist has been known to move small items; it causes pictures to fall off walls and tugs at people's clothing. Another report is in a rather unusual location in Penzance. In September 2003, at the Co-op stores on Queens Square, mysterious footsteps were heard moving around the shop floor; power cuts and items on the shelves moving after closing time have plagued the management. Video footage apparently showed a pack of beer moving itself from the shelves and landing on the floor below. The entity was thought to be an old woman, who had been seen by one staff member – though it was later said the reports were hoaxed by an employee after media attention.

Staff at Meltham shoe shop in Padstow were plagued with extraordinary phenomena in May 2005. Two of the shop workers were terrorised by several poltergeist-like incidents involving a pair of deck shoes. The footwear would jump off the display stand in front of workers and move around at night. A priest was called in to bless the shop but failed to prevent the shoes from moving again. The ghost of a butcher who committed suicide in a nearby cattle shed was blamed for these events.

At the Cornish Arms public house, St Blazey in 2006, a poltergeist enjoyed ringing a bell in the kitchen and pinching the bottoms of female bar and kitchen staff. Voices have also been heard in an empty bar and spectral figures, although not as common, have also been reported here. A clairvoyant who visited the venue identified the entity as a former chef.

The Cornish Arms at St Blazey. The streets here are said to be stalked by a ghostly bear-like creature, which makes a sound more like a horse.

In April 1821 a famous story of extreme poltergeist activity was reported on Carlow Street in Truro: a house was being bombarded with stones that seemed to come from thin air. Neighbours and the town mayor were so alarmed that the army were called out to protect the house. The activity continued for some time, even after the windows and doors were boarded up from the inside. Teapots and dishes were smashed and other household items appeared to move around the kitchen on their own. The owner became very ill so the family moved in with a friend on another street. Strangely, the activity continued; it seemed that the spirit had followed them. Later on a doctor noticed that 'something was not quite right' with the son of the family and 'under duress' the son admitted to faking the activity because his mother had been 'a very stern character' and he wanted to pay her back for all his 'punishment'. This became known as 'Truro's own ghost story' and was published in many newspapers around the UK including the *London Times*. To this day the story is still believed and it is felt that the son had been forced to admit he was the culprit because the townsfolk suspected there was witchcraft involved. During the period of the alleged poltergeist activity, a woman had been beaten and nearly killed by the villagers who assumed she was the cause. It was not long after this nasty event that the son admitted his involvement; however, this does not explain to the many different witnesses how he could have thrown stones, on countless occasions, without being seen.

Poltergeist activity has been reported at the Crumplehorn Inn and Mill, near Polperro. Prior to a change of ownership in the mid-2000s, this charming and delightful building was said to regularly offer visitors and residents unusual experiences; these include the ghost of a young woman and an elderly gentleman. An investigation team did report unexplainable encounters during the course of their stay, which largely matched with the owner's own accounts of ghostly goings on. The sound of a cup being dragged was heard from an empty room upstairs, and a light turned itself off in another before functioning perfectly. Their time downstairs revealed a collection of unusual sounds, including dragging, shuffling and whispering all being heard in the bar, emanating from the restaurant.

Nearby is the Noughts and Crosses, a quaint building dating back to the late sixteenth century. Originally a bakery, it is now a pub and the activity reported was from a previous

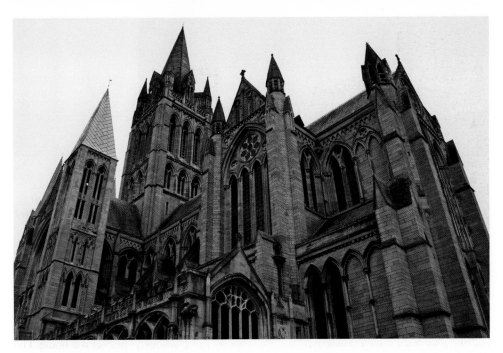

The gothic splendour of Truro Cathedral, the streets of Cornwall's capital city has many ghouls.

stint as a guesthouse. In the upper rooms and stairwell, a strange feeling has been reported, accompanied by the sighting of a small figure. Also reported by a cleaner was the sensation of invisible hands pulling her back from a window she nearly fell out of.

Following a performance of *A Midsummer Night's Dream* set in her back garden in Porthcurno, Rowena Cade began a fifty-year journey to build, largely with her own hands, the Minack Theatre – a most unique and visually stunning open air theatre. The theory held by the daughter of Rowena's first gardener is that she returns to keep an eye on her beloved theatre and, perhaps, has some involvement in causing objects to disappear and re-appear later within the visitor centre. The history of the site stretches back much further, and it is claimed to be built over a former monastery; many still say that the outline of Minack Rock at the base of the theatre looks, at certain times of the day, exactly like the head of a monk wearing a hood.

In July 2007, members of Supernatural Investigations arrived at a confidential location near Redruth. The first real show of activity was in a small room with no windows; there was a single entrance and two motion detector units had been placed in this room facing each other The room was empty, and had been for over forty-five minutes, when suddenly the motion detectors sounded. Two members of the team immediately ran to the room and opened the door – but there was no one there. Later on, the team sat quietly observing for about forty-five minutes; just before the teams were due to swap over, a bang was heard in the corner of the room. It sounded as though something had been thrown. On requesting the same activity, nothing happened. The team decided to revisit this area about an hour later; once again they sat silently for about forty-five minutes with no signs of activity. The minute they stood up to leave, an almighty bang occurred again in the same area of the room. It was a lot louder this time, so much so that one team member jumped and ran two or three steps. At this time a few team members felt a

Minack Theatre, above the waters of Porthcurno Bay.

'rush of wind' move quickly past them and out the door behind them. The other team, located in the hall below, radioed through to ask what the commotion was. They had reported hearing footsteps running the length of the building (which would equate to fourteen or fifteen steps) yet only one team member had moved a few steps. At this point they investigated the area of the room where the bangs had occurred, to see if there was anything untoward that could cause these noises. The team found nothing and proceeded to leave the area. During a later session, near the end of the investigation, a number of the team decided to check this area again. They sat quietly, waiting for something to happen, and again nothing occurred until the team went to leave again. At this point they heard the same banging sound, but this time a lot louder and more aggressive – enough for them to leave in fear for their own safety. This was a spectacular experience for the team and no natural reason could be found for this type of physical activity.

During the evening, in the same location, it seemed as though a chair had moved on its own; they were unable to determine if it had been relocated by another member of the team at some point during the switchover. On listening back to the audio footage, a 'dragging' sound can be heard clearly on tape before a team member comments on the chair's new location.

The ruins of old engine houses litter Cornwall's mining districts, one of which is plagued by a series of poltergeist events.

A view looking towards Trewavas Head, with the engine houses left from the mining activities here clearly visible. With mining being such a dangerous job and the source of many superstitions, it is little wonder we are left with poltergeist reports from some of the buildings involved.

Supernatural Investigations has since revisited the location three times, but the activity has not been the same. As poltergeist activity goes, this was a special occasion. Prior to this, some of the team had also participated in a further three investigations here, two of which produced comparatively little in terms of poltergeist activity. But the second of the three vigils provided an unusual audio encounter, experienced by both Kevin and Stuart from the SI team, along with three others. What follows is an extract from the original report compiled in 2006, and to this day it is one of the most inexplicable cases of poltergeist activity we have ever encountered:

Most of the investigation team had left and with the security of dawn approaching and the light becoming brighter, any feelings of apprehension had vanished completely. There was general discussion of how the night went, along with general chatter amongst friends. However, more strange noises kept happening and at one point a figure or shadow was seen to move past – as indeed someone else had witnessed earlier. As before, there was no one in the area inside or outside; it would be impossible for the external door to have been opened and shut without us seeing and hearing it. We recreated this but the light and noise are unmistakable. The final shock came a few minutes after, when all present heard what sounded like the heavy locked and bolted door being opened upstairs and someone walking around, very loudly. Some of us rushed up there expecting to find a security risk from the living. We covered the area in a blanket of light, from high-powered torches, to find no one outside in the area and both doors shut. We are confident that no one could have come into the area and left without us seeing or hearing them; this was confirmed by those downstairs who heard the original bang, then footsteps, followed by us entering the room (our voices were distinctly recognisable). As we somewhat nervously made our way inside, we found nobody and absolutely no trace of entry or disturbance.

FOUR

FEROCIOUS FELINES, MONSTERS AND MERMAIDS

Nature is full of surprises, especially with animals; genetic development provides us with hybrids and mutations which often lead to what we might call 'giant' versions. Considering the real-life Cornish giant, Anthony Payne (who we discuss later), there is proof that known life forms can exist in substantially larger sizes. The European wildcat has survived in parts of Scotland and cross-bred with domestic cats; their legacy continues in the larger farm cats across south-west England. We have personally encountered some particularly big black farm cats on Bodmin Moor; had their domestic features not been so easily made out to us, we have to admit that, if seen in a different context such as sprawled out on a tree, our analysis might well be different.

So, we can accept that large versions of such animals actually exist within Cornwall, termed as Alien Big Cats or 'ABCs' – could misinterpretation by eyewitnesses really account for the fabled black Beast of Bodmin? We, as humans, often exaggerate, or indeed play down, perceived size based on whether our primal instincts have determined whether such an animal is a physical threat. This is mirrored in feline behaviour; when a cat feels threatened it will instinctively hunch its back up, elongating itself to appear as large as possible and scare off the perceived danger. However, the majority of Big Cat sightings have not been of an up-close nature; often the cat is seen resting, or prowling along, and seemingly unaware of the

Cardinham Woods, on the west side of Bodmin Moor. Big cats have been seen and encountered in the surrounding area.

Does a small colony of leopards or pumas really hunt the south end of Bodmin Moor in times of need, before returning to the more isolated north?

observer. Importantly, the sightings are often made by people with extensive knowledge of the area, hardly people likely to feel excited or wary of new surroundings.

The most famous of Cornish cases is the 'Beast of Bodmin'; the main sightings and associated animal deaths and attacks took place between the mid-1980s and '90s. In October 1993, a woman walking her dogs in the Cardinham area reported being knocked unconscious by a puma-like animal. Her story should not be easily dismissed as police confirmed that there had been at least two recent sheep killings in the area. The author Michael Williams has also had at least one encounter with a large cat, which crossed the road some fifteen metres ahead of him near St Breward in 1993. The accounts from farmers are among the most interesting, due to the physical evidence of their lost livestock. During 1994 at least one sheep farmer retired due to the attacks, and another claimed the loss of a dozen sheep and three calves in this year alone.

Numerous reports have been received over the last ten years, including a spate of livestock deaths and mutilations taking place on the moor in 1999, indeed we have come across such attacks ourselves whilst on Dartmoor, not that far away, during the same year. Big Cats, of course, do not respect man's boundaries, and are capable of travelling the distance between the two counties in a matter of days. All of the large cat species are able to travel up to twenty miles during the course of a single night. The military have been involved in several operations, or training exercises, to try and capture evidence of the beast. None of these have produced evidence that such creatures exist within our countryside, but neither have they proved that they do not. The large distances that such cats naturally roam, combined with a keen instinct to survive and therefore avoid all possible contact with humans, provides a viable explanation as to how any such animal could have evaded the searchers. While the RAF were combing Bodmin Moor, it is feasible that the beast was making its way to another stalking ground. The conspiracy theorists, of course, point out that no full investigation or report has been carried out and made public. Perhaps, as with unidentified flying objects, the military and government see no need to publicly prove what they already believe to exist – why cause potential panic, and bear the financial cost of being seen to deal with the problem, when it is disbelieved by most anyway?

Other theories for the existence of large cats within our countryside include the notion that they are currently undiscovered species, hybrids or prehistoric survivors. One of the more popular theories, which we would agree with combined with the misidentification idea, is that they are escaped or released animals. The Dangerous Animals Act of 1976 is seen as a major reason for owners to release such animals into the wild, rather than have them put down or comply with the costs involved with the act; however, there were significant sightings before this time. Supporters of the 'escaped animals' theory would argue that the animals could have escaped from other sources – travelling circuses, private collections etc. have all existed over the last two centuries. Many large cat skulls, including leopards, have been found across Devon and Cornwall; often these are clearly identifiable by experts, such as the Natural History Museum, as having damage consistent with them being prepared as trophies or rugs. So, little proof of the evidence of Big Cats roaming our countryside – but then, if such predatory creatures do not want to be seen, they won't. Natural history, and indeed evolution, has confirmed this.

A case that adds weight to the theory of misidentification came when north London police were hunting what had been described as a small lioness in Winchmore Hill. Their prey turned out to be a particularly large ginger tom named Bilbo. Misidentification has also occurred in Cornwall; in 1997 a large Abyssinian domestic cat was mistaken for a sunbathing puma. The story made the press and highlights how an oversized domestic animal can fool many into thinking they have encountered, or photographed, an exotic or dangerous creature. Wild cats, Abyssinian cats, the hybrid Kellas cat and the small African lynx (caracal) all exist within Britain and have often been mistaken for larger cats. This echoes along the investigation of any reportedly paranormal event, from sightings of ghosts to strange objects in the sky. A large number of them must surely be ignored, or at least considered as being explainable by simple witness misinterpretation.

Isolated beaches such as Vault beach were extensively used by smugglers (or 'free traders'), now they may form part of a Big Cat's territory. A little along the coast in January 2009 an orangey-brown big cat was sighted near Veryan, not that far from Falmouth.

But this does not neatly explain every encounter or sighting of unusual animals. Perhaps the most interesting of Cornish Big Cats is the China Fleet leopard of Saltash. Between 1993 and '94 there were many sightings of an animal much bigger than a domestic cat or dog – including a sighting by a retired head teacher, made on the China Fleet Country Club golf course. The initial spate of sightings coincided with a decline in the rabbit population, so the club and its members were not unhappy because of the improvements to the greens! Although, presumably they did not enjoy the task of retrieving several sets of back legs from rabbits, found bitten off and discarded. Droppings were also found; identified as those from a large cat – they contained rabbit bones.

On 2 September 1993 at around 11 a.m., ten people (the majority of whom were police officers) in three separate groups all saw what they described as a black 5ft-long cat with a thick tail walk across the course. Night-vision equipment was used by the owners to try and capture indisputable evidence, but they only managed to encounter tracks. Chris Mosier, a zoologist, biologist, and expert on large cats, visited and took part in an investigation. He concluded that some of the larger tracks could be made by leopards, but added that identification was difficult. He further noted how the majority of sightings were between twenty-eight and thirty-five days apart, consistent with the time a leopard or puma would spend prowling their range. While reports of the China Fleet leopard have largely quietened down, there were subsequent reports from Kit Hill and Pillaton, some four miles north-west of Saltash. Chris Mosier summarises below, making this one of the most viable cases of an Alien Big Cat not just within Cornwall, but Britain:

> This whole series of sightings is one of the more convincing I have looked into. An animal appeared on a regular basis in one part of a range, and then seemed to move to a more remote area as it matured. It could indeed, therefore, have been a leopard.

He further identifies the four main areas within Cornwall where Big Cats are encountered and likely to be able to sustain themselves in relative isolation: east Cornwall, north of Saltash up to the edge of the Tamar; the southern edge of Bodmin Moor, from Jamaica Inn to near Siblyback Reservoir; a band from Penzance to Falmouth; and another from St Austell to Lanivet. We would not consider that these are areas to avoid – after all, the likelihood of seeing such a large creature is very slim, so the risk of an attack is very unlikely indeed. Large cats will normally only attack if they are threatened or consider the target as prey.

Recent reports include one from north Cornwall, in late 2008, when a student of natural history photography encountered a large cat while setting up for some shots. A puma is alleged to have been encountered in St Ives Bay, near Hayle, and a Big Cat with a vivid red coat seen west of Mevagissey were both reported during the 1990s.

Other weird creatures found within Cornwall have also been reported; in 2004 there was an alligator sighting in St Blazey which caught the headlines. Recognised as a 2ft-long caiman alligator from the Cayman Islands, the RSPCA were called in, but could find no trace. There have been accounts of smuggled caimans in the past, but it is likely such an animal would die very quickly due to the colder climate. This century has also seen reports of a black puma prowling RAF Mawgan, which was never caught despite the best efforts of the military. At Mylor Bridge, near Falmouth, a large cat with emerald eyes was reported to have approached a stationary car, stared in the window at the occupant and run off into the night.

St Ives Bay at night, viewed from the direction of Hayle – not just home to a relatively recent Big Cat sighting, but also ghostly ships of the past.

An alternative explanation for the Big Cats suggested to be roaming our countryside is that they are actually ghosts of such animals, their spirits presumably trying to find their way home. This theory could be supported by looking at the ancient legends of large dogs such as the 'Black Shuck', 'Padfoot' and 'Barguest'. Cornwall has its own version – the Hound of Penzance – which allegedly only makes an appearance as an omen of death. There may be some historical root in such legends, as often in medieval times, and possibly before, cats were walled into buildings to act as guardian spirits. It was also believed that the first creature to be buried in a graveyard would be forced to act as a guardian against the Devil approaching from the north. One common practice was to inter a large dog near the entrance. With such long-standing traditions, could the Big Cats of today possibly be little more than an altered continuation of such myths?

One of the most bizarre and recent encounters with unknown animals comes from Falmouth, and this time it does not concern a large cat. In February 2009 the *Falmouth Packet* ran a story on a strange kangaroo-like hopping creature, described as 3-4ft high, with big glowing eyes, thick black fur and a long bushy tail. Several further reports were then received from other witnesses, including both current and prior sightings. One published in April 2009 details a similar encounter along the same stretch of coastal path as the original, between Swanpool and Maenporth. The waters of Falmouth Bay have also been the scene for the sighting of a sea serpent in the 1970s, also featured within the pages of the *Falmouth Packet*. Dubbed 'Mowgarw' from the old Cornish for 'Sea Giant', the creature, probably best described as a counterpart to the Loch Ness Monster, was spotted several times –notably from Rosemullion Head and Pendennis Point. As one of the world's largest natural harbours, the area of Falmouth could be appealing to such a large creature as a breeding ground. But surely the substantial traffic of ships in and out of this bustling port would have enabled further sightings? The best place to hope for an encounter is the area between Rosemullion Head and Toll Point, known as 'Morgawr's Mile'.

Other Cornish hotspots for the elusive monsters of the deep include Land's End, where in 1906 the crew of an American ship witnessed a thick snake-like creature with fierce teeth.

The Carrick Roads in Falmouth harbour, viewed from Pendennis Point, scene of not just recent Big Cat and marsupial encounters, but also monsters of the deep.

A chaplain and student in 1907 reported watching a large sea monster swim by the Tintagel area. Further north along the coast is Bude, which has at least two accounts of an unidentifiable creature in its waters from the late nineteenth and early twentieth centuries. There is also an account from 1876 of a serpent being beaten off crabbing lines by two fishermen off Gerrans Bay, Porthscatho. More recently, a pair of green sea beasts, resembling Chinese dragons, were observed off the coast of Looe in 1959. Misidentification could be a reasonable assumption for some of these encounters; in 1933 the body of an unknown sea monster was washed up on Praa Sands beach – it was later proved to simply be a basking shark, in a state of decomposition.

Misidentification by early sailors of the manatee and dugong, along with the washing up of their distorted sea-ravaged corpses, is widely accepted as the source of the myth of the mermaid. However, their origins stem back further to an abundance of fish-tailed deities found throughout man's early cultures. This mutated by the Middle Ages to tales of half-human descendants of primeval ancestors, who chose not to come on land but dwell within the oceans. Perhaps the many travellers to Cornwall, who brought their own folklore with them, added to the existing superstitions of the sea, forging the widely-held belief that merfolk were real and could be treacherous, luring ships onto rocks with their deadly song. This would certainly appear to be a continuation of the ancient Greek myth of Ulysses and the sirens, very real human 'wreckers' later took their place, perhaps it could be due to them and the 'free traders' that we owe the survival of mermaids within Cornish folklore? The eccentric vicar, Robert S. Hawker of Morwenstow (*see* p. 48), is said to have fooled many by posing as a singing mermaid off the coast of Bude by using oilskins and seaweed. His last appearance was marked by a rendition of 'God Save the King', before he disappeared beneath the waves, never to return in 'mer' form again.

The Mermaid of Zennor is Cornwall's, if not Britain's, most famous record of mermaids. It is the tale of how a mermaid was led to the shore by the choir singing in the church at Zennor, and how she became so enchanted by the beautiful voice of Matthew Trevella that

she lured him out to sea. The legend is that his voice can still be heard, when the tides and wind are right, singing below the waves in Pendower Cove. Nearby is 'Witches' Rock', so named after the midsummer rituals carried out here, although it is still considered good luck to touch the stone nine times at midnight. There is certainly a timeless atmosphere to the area, added to, supposedly, by the sight of a man covered in blood frantically cycling down the road as if looking for help, only to disappear into thin air. Many years after Matthew Trevella's disappearance, the legend was added to when a 'merry maid' complained of a ship's anchor blocking her path home to her husband and children in Pendour Cove.

Cudden Point is not only said to be home to mermaids, but also to buried treasure. Sennen Cove, Padstow harbour, and Looe are amongst the many places said to also be frequented by the people of the sea, while in the Scilly Isles, Tresco has 'Piper's Hole', a cave long said to be the haunt of mermaids. There are also rumours of this cave connecting Tresco to the island of St Mary's; legend has it that a dog from Tresco proved this by suddenly appearing from a cave on the shoreline of St Mary's.

The churchyard in Zennor offers some of the most unusual cross designs in the county.

FIVE

INN SEARCH OF SPIRITS

Pubs and inns often have intriguing and mystical pasts due to the age and location of such establishments. Cornish pubs are no different and various ones hold many stories of deception, plotting, shipwrecking and murder. Public houses are renowned for their hosting of social gatherings. This formidable atmosphere creates masses of energy whether it is laughter and enjoyment or sometimes, unfortunately, violence and trouble. It is believed that people will tend to go where they feel most comfortable when they pass over, and for a few, their comfort zone will be sat at the end of the bar in their local ale house. All pubs at one stage or another can report strange goings on – even new ones. However, it is usually the older venues that have the more intriguing tales to tell.

The Albion, Liskeard

One such establishment is the Albion, Liskeard, built in 1905. After various reports from the resident landlord, landlady and the locals, Supernatural Investigations were called to perform an investigation at this historical inn. The landlady and her family had reported many different strange occurrences in the three and a half years they had lived there, which have included distinct smells emanating around the bar and cellar area. It was the smell of cigar smoke which stood out – ironically, it became apparent after the recent smoking ban. Regular bangs and crashes have also been reported coming from this area, along with the swinging of light fittings over the bar, movements of bar furniture and the sound of tapping on the windows. More concerning still was the activity they had reported from their living quarters upstairs – poltergeist activity and actual manifestations in their bathroom. With a teenage boy living at the accommodation, Supernatural Investigations felt it was appropriate to perform an investigation to see if they could shed any light on the situation and possibly help to defuse it.

In a recent interview with the landlady, Sue Lundon, we asked what seemed to be the most notable experience she could remember, she said:

> Probably the strangest event for me was when I came to open up in the morning and found the John Smiths barrel cup link was attached to the larger cup link. The previous evening when we closed they were left correct. Only my husband and I were there at the time. Whatever is here likes to play around in the cellar!

We then asked Sue about her husband's experiences, she said:

My husband was in the bathroom getting ready for bed when he suddenly saw what appeared to be a spiral of water shoot across the room. This seemed to originate in the airing cupboard and shoot across the room and out through the window. This is his only experience.

We asked Sue about the locals and the staff experiences, she continued:

Most of the staff have the feeling that something or someone is standing behind them, but there is no one there. Other locals have experienced the smells and the movement of the lights above the bar. These tend to swing furiously even though no windows or doors are open!

Sue then mentioned an experience her father had while visiting the premises: 'He was up early on a Sunday morning, cleaning, and he heard someone behind him say "Hello". On answering and turning around he was intrigued to find that there was nobody there, it put a chill down his spine!'

When the Supernatural Investigations team arrived at the pub it was still occupied by various locals who all enthusiastically chipped in with their own interesting stories and subjective opinions on the reported occurrences. During the hours the pub was open, efforts were focused upstairs in the living quarters. Regular baseline shots were logged in each of the rooms and then the team split into two for the investigation. An interesting anomaly was caught on video camera in the lounge. Kevin, a member of SI, was standing near a cabinet next to the window. What seemed to be a glowing ball of light moved very steadily and slowly, in a direct straight line, in front of Kevin and then through the near wall. What made this anomaly interesting was that it did not operate in the same way that an insect, dust or other associated natural phenomena would. Upon further investigation there was still no explanation.

Upon investigating the bathroom the team felt uncomfortable and unusually cold. Ironically, this was the smallest, warmest room of the house so these feelings were unexplained. The feeling of something lurking in the cupboard was prominent and the temperature readings seemed to indicate a wind source emanating from this small hole. When the doors were opened, the team were surprised to find this was the airing cupboard and the tank was hot. At that moment, what can only be explained as a rush of wind moved from the airing cupboard, through the team and towards the bathroom window. This was very strange as this cupboard was on an internal wall. Within minutes the room felt comfortable and warm. The bathroom itself is

The Albion, Liskeard.

located over part of the cellar and seemed to tie in with earlier accounts from the family and locals.

The team spent a considerable amount of time in the cellar and this proved a very intriguing location. Kevin and Jason decided to try 'calling out' to see if there would be any response. On asking a question, the outside cellar door seemed to knock a few times. When they repeated the question they received the same response. At this point one of the other investigators went outside to make sure the wind was not causing the door to rattle and to make sure someone wasn't outside. The cellar door leads out into the beer garden which is surrounded by high walls. At this point into the investigation it was approximately 3 a.m.; the investigators were the only ones present. No noises were heard the entire time the investigator was outside; it was a breezy night but the door was silent throughout this period. On his return, questioning continued and the door appeared to knock again in response. This became prominent in the investigation and heavily supported the accounts that had previously been recorded there.

Since this time Supernatural Investigations has visited the property once again, but has found that the activity was more docile. We followed up with Sue to find out if things had got better since the investigations, she said:

Absolutely! Having the team onsite has helped 'move' the negative entities along. We do still get the odd quirky experience but this is nothing compared to the feelings we used to get. I still don't like entering the cellar, particularly on my own; however, I think this is more to do with me than anything that maybe lurking in there!

Smugglers Den Inn, Cubert, near Newquay

Set in a valley, this sixteenth-century thatched inn is well known for its excellent food and wide range of ales; less well known are its other worldly inhabitants. Originally named Trebellan Farm, it is mentioned in the Domesday Book and was occupied by Sir Francis Vivian in 1636. Parish records show that members of the Vivian family were still in residence during the nineteenth century. The current name originated from times of hardship, when it became a hideout for local smugglers and wreckers who forced ships onto the treacherous rocks at nearby Holywell Bay to gain some of their precious cargo. Under the 'Royalty of Wrecks', the lord of the manor was entitled to keep the merchandise for himself, thus forcing the smugglers

The sign at the Smugglers Den.

The quaint courtyard and thatched roof of the Smugglers Den.

Not far from the Smugglers Den is the thirteenth-century Treguth Inn, previously a farmhouse, tearoom and private club. Shadowy figures and poltergeist activity was experienced for a while.

to steal some contraband for themselves. In 2006 several of the team took part in a full-scale investigation, Kevin Hynes describes in his own words a most startling experience:

> I was talking to Stuart in the main bar when I asked did he see anyone go in to the toilets, as the corridor was directly in front of us and the toilets were to the right of the corridor. Stuart looked around and all the team were accounted for in the bar area. I can only describe what I saw as a dark figure from the shoulder area down walking into the toilet area.

In all the years we have been working with Kevin, this is one of only two such reports from him; he is not a man prone to rashly crying out that he has seen someone who isn't there. This account matched closely with the previous reports; many of the previous encounters have been in the corridor by the cloakrooms. Phantom footsteps were also heard by the team from behind the empty bar – we found out later that this is a common experience. While preparing for the drive home, Stuart saw what appeared to be a dark figure moving past the window upstairs. This was out of the corner of his eye at first, but remained for a few seconds when he turned round to face the window in question. It was now very late in the night (or early in the morning, depending on how you look at it), but a lot of the team had reported shadows etc. throughout the second half of the night. With the building now locked we were unable to return and verify if someone was walking around. A shame, really, as this pub was the setting for a higher-than-normal collection of visual encounters during an investigation. It begs the question: was the entire team tired and experiencing corner-of-the-eye phenomena? Or were we really seeing the ghosts of Smugglers Den?

First and Last Inn, Sennen, near Land's End

Kevin Hynes and Stuart took part in an investigation and preliminary visits, covered by ITV Westcountry, at the First and Last back in 2005. The team experienced shadows, knocking and footsteps while upstairs, all in line with previous reports. Parts of the inn date back as far as the thirteenth century and there are rumours of secret tunnels dug under the inn by those smuggling booty; there is some evidence to support this, or at least provide an origin to such myths, in the shape of 'Annie's Well'. The glass cover to this forms part of the floor within the inn and it takes an uneasy couple of steps to cross it. Back in the 1800s the First and Last was run by Joseph and Annie George, who blackmailed Dionysius Williams into letting them live there rent free in return for keeping quiet about Williams' smuggling business – no mean feat as Joseph was apparently his smuggling agent. Eventually they were removed from the inn. Annie, in a fit of rage, then turned against him and several others by turning evidence against Williams, who served a long prison sentence. Her brother-in-law, John George, is said to have been hanged for his part. The story doesn't conclude there for Annie, who had a far from happy ending. The local villagers sought revenge for the betrayal and she was staked out on Sennen Beach at low tide, before being dragged down by fishing nets as the water rose above her. One of the bedrooms above the inn still bears her name, and it is from within here that her spirit is said to roam, having been laid here before being consigned to an unmarked grave. Various landlords have reported seeing a lady on the landing, finding cats shut in wardrobes and drawers

The First and Last at Sennen, Britain's most westerly village. The scene of smugglers and wreckers since the 1600s, here was possibly the origin of 'Watch the wall my darling, while the gentlemen go by', as villagers were advised to see nothing, so they were not lying if questioned by authorities.

and experiencing chills, cold spots and the sensation of being touched. Others have reported dreams of drowning and of being covered in fishing nets; it would seem that Annie does not like others being in her room. The landing certainly has a strange feel to it and Stuart confessed to being glad to leave after he had completed a lone vigil here.

Kevin and Stuart returned almost a year later, in autumn 2006. They had requested to take another look around after the newly appointed management couple left the weekend before – in the middle of their first night! From interviewing some of the staff and regulars, we learnt that a séance had been held in the bar and that numerous phenomena had been experienced both during and after, including a reported fifteen sightings! The couple who left have since avoided contact with Land's End so we were unable to interview them or gain any further details. We did, however, speak to several of the staff who were present and their own opinions were a little mixed – we couldn't help but leave thinking that the alleged paranormal activity could be, at least in part, due to the nervous disposition and perhaps overactive imagination of a couple in strange surroundings. That said, it doesn't fully explain all of the accounts reported to us, and from the first investigation and our own on this night, there was definitely something amiss at the First and Last.

The Gweek Inn, Gweek, near Helston

Previously the subject of local media, both on Radio Cornwall and Westcountry TV, strange happenings at the Gweek Inn appear to have quietened down of late. Our colleague, Kevin

The Gweek Inn. The history of Gweek as a port stretches back to Roman times. The Tudor period saw it with its own customs house.

Hynes, was present for an investigation in October 2004 and recalls his first impressions of the inn to be a warm and friendly environment, found a stone's throw away from the head of the Helford River. Shadowy figures have been witnessed in one of the bedrooms, the lounge, the bar and entering the restaurant. Poltergeist activity has also been experienced in the bar and bedroom. Although Kevin reports that contact was made with some of the inn's former residents by a psychic during his visit, there was little in the way of sightings or poltergeist activity experienced. He did admit to a very strong feeling of being watched, though – which just wouldn't go away – while he was in the bar. Almost as if someone was staring intensely at him from within the restaurant, even though it was empty!

William IV, Truro

Situated in Kenwyn Street, this former hotel now trades as a pub and restaurant. Thought to have been built on the site of a former Dominican friary, the ghostly figure of a friar or monk has been seen over the years. Subsequent faiths or religious institutions were often built near or over the sites of their predecessors; the pub's proximity to the imposing Truro Cathedral would support these claims. There have also been sightings of shadowy figures at a field on the outskirts of the city. Known as Comprigney (derived from the Cornish *gwel cloghprenyer*: 'the field of the gibbet'), rattling chains are also said to be heard here once night has fallen. It is an area still said to be avoided by locals during the hours of darkness.

The William IV in Cornwall's capital. Not far from here is the ghost of a murdered girl, glimpsed in Castle Street at a now closed inn.

The Bucket of Blood, Phillack, near Hayle

A very old pub complete with low beams and ceilings; the name and the gruesome depiction on its sign come from an old murder linked to smugglers. The story is that the landlord drew a bucket from the well to find the water turned red with blood; a mutilated body, believed to be a local revenue man, was then discovered in the well. While the origins of this tale have been partly obscured with the passing of time, an apparition of a man has been reported dripping wet and dressed in ripped clothes.

The Bucket of Blood is said to be haunted by a phantom monk.

The Dolphin, Penzance

Unusual feelings and poltergeist activity have been experienced here, especially the loud, heavy footsteps which regularly plague the staff and residents. Heard from both within the cellar and the bar, it is said to be a distinct plod along the wooden floors, and never is there anyone to account for them. Much of this phenomena is attributed to the often-sighted ghost of a sailor wearing a tricorn hat, who is said to have been hanged for a petty crime; also credited is a real-looking man with very white-blond hair, regularly encountered in the cellar.

Some evidence has been found to confirm the rumoured smugglers' tunnels which run under the pub, and it is said that the cellar ghost is a man who unfortunately fell to his death during the eighteenth century.

The Dolphin is one of Cornwall's oldest inns; the bar was previously used as a courtroom.

Many areas of Penzance are allegedly home to ghosts, including the churchyard of St Mary's Church. Not only is it unusual to find a well-reported account from a graveyard, but the graveyard is also unique in Britain as its foliage is predominantly made up of palm trees. Part of the path of steps leading to the church is said to have been the site of a former cholera pit; strange groaning sounds have been heard nearby along with the sighting of a sinister white figure described as gliding between the trees. These reports have been made over a long period of time, from completion of the church in 1832 until the twenty-first century, as recently as 2001 people were troubled enough by what they had experienced to write in to the local newspapers.

Bush Inn, Morwenstow

Bush Inn is immortalised by the famous Cornish poet, Revd Hawker, as the lair of many a wicked and evil smuggler and wrecker – notably, and a little before his time, Cruel Coppinger. A particularly nasty and unpleasant individual, he arrived at Welcombe Mouth in 1792, the only survivor of a wrecked Danish ship. Ghost stories at the Bush Inn may originally have been invented by its less reputable visitors as a means of keeping others, including the revenue men, away. Although, the sighting of a man at the foot of the stairs persists until the current day, presumed to be one of many unknown sailors washed up on the beaches nearby. The cut-throat reputation of Coppinger's band of brigands was such that they probably did not need to do much to feed the legends; the gruesome death count of those involved, many missing never to be seen again, may have accomplished this alone.

The ghost of Revd Hawker is said to be heard in the form of phantom footsteps around his old church in Morwenstow. The Bush Inn is also regarded by many as the inspiration for Daphne Du Maurier's *Jamaica Inn*, the celebrated writer having visited while staying in Kilkhampton. It is the only inn along the wrecker's coast from Bude to Hartland Point, so there may be some truth in this; either way, the inn has been the centre of legends and ghost stories for several hundred years.

Other pub ghosts in Cornwall ...

We could never hope to include a round up of all the haunted pubs in Cornwall within this book, but there are many more, including: the Royal Standard, Gwinear, near Hayle, which in 2006 saw reports of disembodied footsteps and other strange noises; the King's Head at Altarnun, said to still be visited by one of its former landladies, Peggy Bray; the Three Pilchards, said to be named after the three pilchard curers who offered tasting at Polperro's oldest inn – the *Cornish Times* ran an article which included an account of one of the owners, amongst others, who had witnessed the figure of a woman upstairs and in the backyard, one time apparently milking a cow; and the Ship Inn at Mousehole, home to the spectre of a man who appears to be real but simply disappears. A strange smell of violets has also been reported within the bar.

Additionally, the Manor House Inn at Rilla Mill, set on the edge of Bodmin Moor, has been the home of phantom footsteps, heard coming from upstairs – the sounds are always traced back to an empty bedroom. The author Michael Williams describes how he believes the Crow's Nest Inn, also on the edge of Bodmin Moor, to be genuinely haunted by at least four different ghosts – including a woman who sadly waits in vain for her lover to return from the nearby mines, another lady who returns for a drink, a gentleman who disappears through a wall in the bar, and ghostly footsteps which are heard coming from upstairs.

SIX

LEGENDS AND PISKIES

Fairy legends exist all over the Celtic/Gaelic land. There are widespread stories of these 'beings' throughout Scotland, Wales, Ireland and England. A famous story exists in West Yorkshire regarding the Cottingley fairies, in which fairies were allegedly captured on a still camera. This made the news in the early 1900s. More information on this can be found in *Paranormal West Yorkshire* by Andy Owens. With regards to Cornwall, this county has an abundance of history relating to 'small people', most of which has been written about by Robert Hunt in his work *Popular Romances of the West of England* published in 1865. It is probably sensible to open this chapter with a segment from another of his works, *Cornish Fairies*, in which he mentions that there are five different types of the 'fairy family' in Cornwall: 'the small people', 'the spriggans', 'piskies or pigseys', 'The bucca, bockles or knockers' and 'the browneys'.

He explains that the 'Small People are believed by some to be the spirits of the people who inhabited Cornwall many thousands of years ago – long, long before the birth of Christ.' These are a friendly, playful race who attempt to aid people to whom they take a fancy. Spriggans are often thought to be 'offshoots of Trolls and are found in cairns, quoits, cromlechs burrows or detached stones'. They are mischievous characters with a thieving nature and were usually blamed for the disappearance of children or cattle from homes or farms. Piskies too are mischievous fairies with an ignorant, unsociable streak. They used to play many a trick on the wanderers of the moors. It was thought that if you wore your coat inside out you became immune to the piskie magic. The knockers or tinners (as they are also known), are well-known sprites of the mines; they are believed to be the souls of the Jews who used to work the tin-mines in Cornwall. Richard Holland from Uncanny UK expands:

> Cornwall has a particularly rich folklore regarding mine fairies. They were rarely seen but, as in other parts of the UK, more usually heard; for they too would be working the mines and the sounds of their digging would indicate the location of the best sources of ore … They seemed well disposed towards their human counterparts and never seemed to resent the fact that they led them to the richer lodes … However, like all of their kind, it was unwise to deal selfishly with the knockers or to try and cheat them. One old story tells of a Cornish tin miner who struck a bargain with the knockers to allow him to work a rich lode they had found, if he would return to them just 10 per cent of the washed and dressed ore … all went well until the old fellow died and his son took over. Perhaps he did not believe in the knockers; at any rate, he resented returning the meagre fraction back to the workings and kept it all for himself.

Skeletal reminders of Cornwall's mining heritage and the customs of miners, including leaving gifts of food for the 'knockers' or 'tinners' and rewarding snails that made their way down with candle wax.

Immediately, the lode failed, nothing went right with him again, bitter and disappointed, he took to drink and ultimately died a beggar.

Finally, Robert Hunt explains the fifth type of fairy as a browney. Apparently this is a sprite attached to a household who devotes his every care to the resident family; they are guardians to the landlord and their family and can be very protective. The browneys are reported to be small, solitary, shaggy-haired domestic sprites, which are said to do chores around the home. In *Cornish Fairies*, they are summoned to assist with a swarm of bees:

When this occurs, mistress or maid seizes a bell-metal or a tin pan, and, beating it, she calls 'Browney, Browney' as loud as she can until the good Browney compels the bees to settle.

Looking out from within the twenty-metre long fogou at Carn Euny near Sancreed; appearing above the ground, it is easy to see why such sites are nicknamed 'pixie houses'.

Many strange lights have been witnessed on or near the rocks of Carn Kenidjack, also said to be the lair of Old Moll and her witches.

Constantine is home to 'Pixie's Hall', an underground, earth covered, stone tunnel with chambers leading off, known as a fogou. Derived from the Celtic, 'Ifócw' and Cornish, 'fogo' both meaning cave, they are also known as 'fuggy-holes' in Cornwall. Often associated with the little people or piskies (the holes are thought to be their homes) they are actually most likely Iron Age burial chambers. Many still exist, scattered across the South West. Close to Garras, south of Helston, is one of the best: Halliggye Fogou. Chyauster Ancient Village and Carn Euny also contain partially surviving examples; disturbingly, many such sites now have some associations with modern witchcraft and the occult.

One of our favourite sites associated with the little people is Carn Kenidjack, an isolated rocky outcrop in the rough moorland area of Pendeen, locally known as 'The Hooting Cairn'. One other legend associated with it is of two miners who, passing by late at night, were joined by a horseman dressed all in black. The rider revealed himself as the Devil, so they were too terrified to refuse his offer of watching a wrestling match on the summit. They found demons fighting, one throwing another against one of the large rocks surrounding the cairn. The two miners sensed the demon was dying and so whispered a prayer in his ear. A black cloud then consumed the demonic party in its entirety, and the ground shock ferociously as they returned underground to the 'gump' below. There are stories of locals avoiding the area at night as strange lights have been witnessed, along with the sense of being watched, and perhaps joined, by unseen forces. There is a serene feeling here, which makes for mostly pleasant visits. However, we have certainly encountered a sudden change in atmosphere here, stronger than any natural change in the weather; but, perhaps thankfully, we have never encountered any piskies or the demons said to linger in its shadow. Nearby is the 'Men-an-tol', a round granite stone with a circular hole surrounded by two standing stones. Also associated with supernatural forces, children were made to crawl through here nine times against the sun to be cured of most diseases, especially rickets.

Some believe fairies exist in their own right; others believe that they are ghosts or spirits of the dead. It was widely believed that if you could see, hear, touch or communicate with the fairies then you were of devil mind. The people claiming such abilities were classed as witches and usually burnt or drowned due to their confessions. One story that reflects this belief is the fascinating experience of Ann Jefferies in the seventeenth century.

Ann Jefferies was born in Cornwall in a little parish called St Teath in 1626. Her education was like many others at this time and she was unable to read or write. It is believed that although this was the case, she was bright and intelligent. Unfortunately, if you were poor in those days, such skills had little opportunity to flourish. Ann was the daughter of a hardworking labourer, an occupation that brought little money. She was fascinated by the curious world of piskies and fairies and often wandered the green land after dark looking for such creatures. On turning nineteen years of age Ann left to work as a servant for a wealthy family; it was here that she met her master's son, Moses Pitt. It is from his recorded account, in letters to the Right Reverend Father in God, Dr Edward Fowler, Lord Bishop of Gloucester, that we learn the most about Ann and her experiences.

Her amazing story began while she sat knitting in the garden one day. As recounted by the Pitt family, she was later found here writhing around on the garden path. She was immediately retrieved and carried to her bedroom where her fit continued and she remained in a type of coma for a while. Eventually she came round and, when the Pitt family asked what had happened to her, she began telling them a story that was quite literally 'out of this world'. Whether she recounted a dream, or a vision of sorts, her story of meeting 'the little people' will remain in people's minds forever. In her story she claimed she had been approached by six little men dressed in green outfits who clambered about her body. Once they reached her neck they set about kissing and caressing her until one covered her eyes. At this point she felt a sharp pain and had the feeling that she was flying. Eventually she felt herself land and, after an exclamation from one of the six tiny men, she opened her eyes. Ann later claimed to have been brought to a mystical and magical land where human-sized people lived.

There were castles and temples everywhere surrounded by gorgeous gardens and lakes; everybody was dressed in gowns and beautifully coloured dresses. She felt at home there and was enjoying this amazing experience. It was not long before her fairy friends returned and, after spending some time with one of the six little men, the other five returned with what she described as an 'angry mob'. For some reason they began attacking their own kind and wounded the little man who was sat with Ann. Immediately her eyes were closed again and she felt herself floating through the air before ending back up in front of the arbour in the garden.

What seems interesting about Ann's story is that you can correlate some parts of her experience to what was physically happening to her while she was in this state. The feeling of flying could be associated with her being carried to her bedroom, the human-sized people could be the Pitt family surrounding her bed and the vision of palaces and temples most probably could be attributed to other items in the room. Maybe she had an old dolls' house or her walls were painted like the Sistine Chapel. However, even though we could link a lot of her dream to natural occurrences, what is strange are the events that follow on from her experience.

According to Moses Pitt, Ann had changed dramatically and rejected food, explaining that she was being kept alive by the 'little men' from her hallucination. More amazing still was her apparent new-found skill of healing and clairvoyance, which she continually performed, successfully, on many different people from all over the land. She would even describe the exact identification of the people who would be coming to see her. Unfortunately, such skills were not ignored during this age where witchcraft was considered a genuine threat and the unknown was deeply feared. She was unfortunately noticed by the Justice of the Peace in Cornwall, John Tregeagle, and imprisoned at Bodmin Jail for a whole three months without food or water, apparently thought to be in league with the Devil and evil spirits. For a further three months she was kept, again with no food or water, at the 'house of the Mayor of Bodmin'. She was eventually released, astoundingly, in very good health, explaining that this was possible because the fairies had kept her well nourished.

Due to her incarceration at Bodmin Jail, she was forbidden to enter or live in the Parish of St Teath again and was forced to work and live in Padstow for an aunt of Moses Pitt. She was reported to be alive many years later after marrying and moving to Devon. She never spoke about her incident again, fearing that she would be returned to Bodmin Jail, or worse, executed!

Many accept that the origins of giant folklore within Cornwall largely stem from the smaller Celts viewing the taller Anglo-Saxons as such, but their myth remains alive in the places associated with them. Lamorna has Giant's Cave, Land's End has Giant's Chair, and of course, the giant Comoran of Mount's Bay. The Cheesewring is a spectacular natural rock formation on Bodmin Moor. It was said to have been made by giants stacking the stones in a game against St Tue, who won with the assistance of an angel, allowing him to place the final stone on top. Another of our favourites is the ancient rock formation of Giant's Cradle on Trecobben Hill, said to be where victims of giants were dragged, murdered and presumably consumed.

It is said that the giant, Bolster, could stand with one foot on Carn Brea, with the other reaching over six miles to St Agnes Beacon. Legend tells of how, after terrorising the countryside, he fell in love with the beautiful missionary St Anne. In order to avoid his affections, she declared that he must fill a hole in the rocks of Chapel Porth with his blood to win her heart. Bolster is then said to have done so, not realising that the hole actually went out to sea, bleeding himself to death. The cliffs at Chapel Porth still bear a red stain as evidence of the legend.

Carn Brea is one of the major signal beacons, and has the custom of the Midsummer Bonfire. Some believe the fires used to symbolise worship of the sun, others suggest it was to drive out witches and spirits.

However, a real life Cornish giant did exist: 7ft 6in Anthony Payne, bodyguard to the Grenvilles during the Civil War. Having lived and died at his master's manor at Stratton, the building, now the Tree Inn, was said to have been significantly altered to allow the giant's huge coffin to be carried in and out.

Said to be home to a ghostly procession of monks, the 40ft waterfall at St Nectan's Glen cascades onto a circular rock, known as the Kieve. It is beneath here that the dying saint threw his silver chapel bell and was later buried in a chest along with a sacramental plate. Many have tried to recover this legendary treasure, without success, including miners who abandoned their quest on hearing a silver bell ring. The hermitage cell is now a shrine below the owner's house, and is seen by many as a place of pilgrimage. During our visits we have encountered the sensation of a woman rushing out from the shrine; she is believed to have been a previous visitor fleeing after being terrified by the apparition of monks walking down the original steps within, which now lead to nowhere.

Dating from the crusades and pronounced 'Trove', Trewoofe Manor, Bosava has rumours of a ghostly spinning maid. She was allegedly bricked up in a room, then released years later by a worker who had been disturbed by noises from behind the wall. The ghosts of two children who drowned in a millpond have reportedly been spotted picking flowers, re-enacting their last happy moments before tragedy struck.

Also associated with Trewoofe is the 300-year-old account of Squire Lovelis, who chased a white hare into a cave at Boleigh. He was later found in a disturbed state, singing wildly of

The shrine inside the hermitage cell of St Nectan's Glen. A smaller version of Madron's Prayer Tree can be seen, along with the original stone steps, covered in velvet.

The area near Trewoofe, pronounced 'Trove'. Versions of this legendary 'wild hunt' have Squire Lovelis as both the quarry and hunt leader.

his encounter with a witch who had changed shape from the hare and introduced her coven leader, a demon. Through Lovelis' ramblings, it was discovered that this demon had taken the guise of a stranger who had earlier seduced his wife. The squire swore at the demon in a fit of rage, whereupon the coven turned on him, resulting in his demented condition. Although we have not encountered his spectre, it is said that he eternally leads his pack of dogs on a 'wild hunt' around the woods and roads of the district.

Atop Roche Rock sits St Michael's Chapel, which dates from 1409; sitting above a previous hermitage cell, it is said to be the retreat of a leper. It casts a dominating presence, even in the shadow of the great china clay works. It is a thought-provoking place to be by day, but altogether eerie and sinister at night. Another Cornish 'wild hunt' legend, of the ill-fated Jan Tregeagle who was pursued across Bodmin Moor by a pack of headless hell hounds, is set here. Seeking sanctuary in the mysterious chapel on Roche Rock, Tregeagle's head alone made it through the window and his body was ravaged by the beasts. This legendary figure actually existed in the 1600s; a hated local magistrate, his crimes in life saw his soul eternally doomed. Tregeagle's spirit can still be encountered on the bleak expanse of Bodmin Moor as he toils to complete a series of impossible tasks. One such task is to empty Dozmary Pool with a limpet shell, rumoured to be bottomless and with a whirlpool at its centre; both of these myths have been dispelled by the pool drying up on occasion. There is an air of mystery still surrounding this large expanse of water, which always seems to be shrouded in some form of mist or cloud. At least during any visits we have made. It is said to be where Sir Percival (or Sir Bedivere, depending on the version) cast the legendary sword of kings, Excalibur, into its depths to be grasped and returned to the guardian spirit, the Lady of the Lake.

Roche Rock was featured in the film Omen III, *which sees two priests pursuing Damian, trapped in (fabricated, they are definitely not there!) dungeons below.*

The formations of rocks at Roche further add to the sense of mystery, reminiscent of a temple or prehistoric site. (Photograph kindly provided by Becky Andrews)

SEVEN

BODMIN JAIL

Bodmin Jail, now a tourist attraction, is partially in ruins. The building displays small exhibits featuring imprisoned offenders and offers a grim view of the criminal culture of Cornwall in days gone by. Originally built in 1779, it became the first modern prison of its kind built in England. Prior to this, the only other gaols in the county were located at Launceston, Falmouth, Truro, Penzance, Lostwithiel and Penryn. These were not big gaols and could only hold a handful of felons or debtors at a time. Bodmin Jail was built according to the reformist ideas of John Howard, a philanthropist. He had suffered extreme cruelty at the hands of a French privateer after being captured *en route* to Lisbon in 1755. Based on his experiences, he wanted to reform the current prison regime and put forward his own innovative ideas as to the future designs.

Although life within the gaol was less harsh than previous prisons, hard labour was still the treatment recommended for a large number of its inmates. The treadmill was a particularly detested and demoralising punishment.

The approach to Bodmin Jail.

Naval quarters at Bodmin Jail.

Nonetheless, our interest is not specifically about the building itself, but more about the people who were incarcerated there. In 1779 there were just under thirty people residing at the prison. By 1830 this number had reached nearly 170. Overcrowding was rife and many people suffered illness and death. With regards to loss of life in the prison which cannot be attributed to the sentence given, there were only seventeen spanning seventy-two years. This is significantly low, given the total population of the prison during this period, which stood at approximately 7,000. Deaths attributed to execution were high; during the 1770s, 241 offences were punishable by hanging. Between 1779 and 1909 there were a total of fifty-six hangings; fifteen of these were for murder the rest were for crimes such as arson, highway robbery, burglary, sheep stealing and bestiality.

Between 1785 and 1802 hangings took place on Bodmin Common, later to become St Lawrence's county asylum; the misery and suffering endured on this site started before the foundations were even laid.

There are rumours from the Second World War that important artefacts, such as the Domesday Book, were hidden in the prison and, somewhat less likely, the Crown Jewels. The jail is even more spectacular from a paranormal investigator's point of view. The place is buzzing with energy and everything within this building is competing to tell its own individual story.

Matthew Weekes, aged twenty-three, was executed for the murder of Charlotte Dymond in 1844. He is believed to have killed his lover in a fit of rage. Nearly 20,000 people turned out to watch his execution – one of the largest crowds ever to grace the hangman's stage. It is believed that Weekes haunts the gaol because he is innocent and another jealous admirer killed Charlotte by a stream below Roughtor on nearby Bodmin Moor, and it is here that her ghost has been spotted. Roughtor itself is regarded as having a special presence and a spine-chilling atmosphere. It is rumoured that, amongst others, the infamous Aleister Crowley conduced macabre midnight rituals at its summit..

Selina Wadge is another inmate who graced the walls of Bodmin Jail. She was one of only four women to be executed at Bodmin, convicted of the murder of her own child. Selina had two children; Henry, also known as Harry, was two years old and John was six. Selina was not married but was reported to be in a relationship with a soldier named James Westwood. Unfortunately, Selina was very poor and was regularly working at the Launceston Workhouse to earn what crust she could for herself and her two sons. Her story begins in 1878 when she was on her way to visit her mother in Alternun (about eight miles from where she was working). It was believed that she was going to meet up with her apparent boyfriend, James Westwood. Reportedly, they had met only twice previously and James had agreed, via letter, to meet her this time. Even though another letter was received after this date stating that he was unable to make the trip to see her, Selina still decided to take her two boys and hitch a ride to Launceston

to meet him. She managed to catch a lift with a local farmer and apparently told him that she was going to meet her boyfriend. She had planned to return to the workhouse that same Friday evening – but she never made it.

It was midday the following day before Selina returned to the workhouse, and she was only accompanied by her older son, John. Selina claimed that her boyfriend James had drowned Harry in a well and threatened to kill her and her other son. John accidentally let slip to the workhouse nurses that same day that his mum had put Harry into a pit. Due to the inconsistency in the stories, the workhouse master immediately sent for the police and Selina was taken into custody where she repeated her same story under caution. Harry's body was found in 3ft of water at the bottom of a deep well in Mowbray Park.

Following this, Selina was arrested, whereupon she told another story regarding the killing of Harry. She claimed that James had threatened not to marry her if she did not kill Harry. James later recounted that he had no 'ill feelings' towards her children. She came before the courts on 27 July 1878, where other colleagues and workmates explained that Selina was a loving mother of good character. The jury deliberated and found Selina guilty of murder, although recommended that 'mercy' be shown in sentencing, due to her kind and loving nature. The mercy shown by the judge was to sentence Selina to death by hanging in Bodmin.

Selina ended her days in the condemned cell where she was kept company by the chaplain. Selina was terrified about the hanging because she thought she would be strangled to death, a very slow and painful way to die. She was not aware that a new law of hanging had been passed which involved the drop platform. Obviously still not a very nice way to die, but a quick and clean death could be expected. They calculated a drop of 8ft for Selina and it was reported by the press later that 'she died without a struggle' once the platform dropped.

Apparently James had written Selina a letter which she had received before her execution asking for 'forgiveness'. When this letter was read to her she was reported to forgive him, although she mentioned that he had a 'lot to ask forgiveness for'. This is very strange and does stir up thoughts as to what he was asking for forgiveness for. Was he really involved with Harry's death? Could it have been an accident?

Stockade area of the jail showing orbs – probably dust.

Selina is allegedly buried in the prison grounds and is one of the spirits that has been witnessed at Bodmin Jail. She is known to tug on clothes and attempt to hold the hands of children when they visit the jail itself. She has also been seen by children who ask 'who is the lady in the white dress who is sobbing?'

Another famous recorded spectre that walks the damp and dreary corridors of Bodmin Jail is reported to be that of Elizabeth Cummins; she was executed by hanging in August 1828 aged just twenty-two. The story explains how, after giving birth out of wedlock, this servant attempted to quieten her baby by covering his face with a blanket. When the baby continued screaming, she attempted once more to silence him by banging his head against the side of the cot. This worked and the baby was quiet; unfortunately too quiet, as he had been killed in the process.

Another lady who once resided at Bodmin Jail was Ann Jefferies (*see* p. 52-3). Ann Jefferies was ordered by Bodmin's High Court to be starved until she confessed that she was a witch. Her survival at Bodmin Jail without nourishment for three months was cause for much speculation and furore; it was even suggested that she had supernatural powers. She revealed her health was due to the regular food brought to her by fairies; this simply furthered people's belief that she was a witch.

There are many stories behind the fifty-six hangings that took place at Bodmin; we are only interested in the ones that have a haunting history at the infamous jail. An abundance of investigations have been performed at the jail over the years, including Living TV's *Most Haunted* along with the Paranormal Site Investigators team (PSI). The majority of the groups seem to collect the same type of evidence, both scientifically and psychically. Similar events experienced consist of small stones being thrown; audio phenomena of rattling keys, grunts and whispering; revolving mist; discernible smells; the feeling of being touched; having your hand clasped or being pushed; and objects that seemingly moving on their own.

In October 2009 Supernatural Investigations were invited to conduct an investigation. Taken from the Bodmin Jail report, the following extract shows that strange things began almost immediately for Stuart and Jason, as Stuart articulates:

> While standing in the basement of the jail at the far left, our attention was with Mark Rablin, our guide for the evening. He was talking about the areas without revealing any pertinent information when suddenly Jason and I looked at each other. We had both felt a strange and overwhelming feeling; within seconds I felt something grab my hand, almost like a little hand. Obviously nothing was there and this was not something I am used to, this was one of the first times this had happened to me … I was speechless.

At the end of the tour the team were returning back to the 'base room' when the following happened as Jason explains:

> During the initial tour of the building, Stuart and I were descending the stairs between the 3rd and 2nd floor. I was descending with a KII EMF meter that has lights to depict when high levels of EMF are close. Usually it is strange for this meter to light up any more than one

Some of the tools we use for paranormal investigations.

Cells on the fourth level.

green light (to show it is on); however, on this occasion, the meter went crazy and all lights were flashing from green to red. I stopped dead in my tracks and called Stuart back (who had been walking in front of me), I moved the meter around and towards some electrics that were located on the wall beside me. When I moved the meter away the lights were still constant. Whatever direction I moved this meter, the lights continued to flash. Within a minute the lights faded and only the initial green light was displayed. I began to follow the route I had used when waving the device before to see if I could recreate the effect. This was not to be the case. The KII meter remained on [for] the rest of the eight-hour investigation, but never reacted in the same way again.

Some very interesting information was picked up psychically. It is worth bearing in mind that Supernatural Investigation's 'sensitives' know very little about the locations they visit, in order to avoid information contamination. While it was amazing that the main ghost characters of the prison were named and their crimes described, what became more interesting was the variation between the stories that were revealed to us and the published, known histories of these crimes. One of the members picked up on a man named 'Matthew' who had been 'hung for murder'; this was assumed to be Matthew Weekes. He went on to say that he could see the man 'stabbing a woman, she was wearing a white dress'. What was interesting is that the investigator said that he was 'angry' because he got caught, and he had an 'accomplice' who had managed to get away with it. He haunts the jail because he wants to tell people that 'there was someone else involved'. It was later revealed to this investigator that Matthew had declared himself innocent of the murder and claimed that another jealous admirer of Charlotte had been responsible.

In another twist of psychic revelation, the same investigator picked up on the presence of a woman, 'Liz', in the basement. He said that he could see her 'sobbing' in the corner. He revealed that she had been executed for 'killing her little boy'. This story seemed to fit in with the tale of Elizabeth Cummins who had murdered her newborn son. At this point it was mentioned that on the wall behind him was a display board detailing the story of Elizabeth Cummins. The basement was pitch black so there was no way that this could have been read; however, the lights were illuminated for the initial tour. It is possible that the information had been read subconsciously during this period. The main twist in this report was that on reading the information thoroughly, the investigator immediately shook his head, saying, 'that's not how it happened.' He mentioned that the display seemed to portray Elizabeth as a murderer, but he could not see how this was true. The story didn't seem to make sense and it was as though Elizabeth was trying to tell him this. He continued to ask another team member, 'If she murdered her own son, why is she sobbing in the corner being comforted by another inmate? At most, this was a tragic accident!'

During a break in the investigation, one of the team members retreated to the naval wing of the prison to get a picture. As it was dark, the camera was set to a thirty-second exposure, set on a tripod and left to run. About fifteen seconds into the exposure, a small stone hit the investigator on the head before it dropped to the ground. When the investigator looked up he was surprised to see that there was nothing located directly above him, apart from open sky; it was as though the stone had been launched from a cell on the third or fourth floor above him. Unless you have a long ladder, there is no access to these cells.

Overall, our investigation at Bodmin Jail was amazing. Just like previous teams, Supernatural Investigations collected some excellent scientific, personal and psychic information to take away and digest. A must for any paranormal enthusiast!

EIGHT

UFOS (THEY COME IN PEACE)

Unidentified Flying Objects, or UFOs as they are more often known, have caused speculation and media interest for thousands of years. 'Wheels in the sky' have even been documented in the Bible. They are often associated with military 'cover-ups' and fall into the category of 'government conspiracies'. This subject alone has been written about in many, many different books, newspapers and even made into films. It covers a vast arena from the silver saucers seen flying high, through to the sightings of little green men, alien abductions, foreign implants and crop circles.

On 29 December 2007, Kelvin Barbery was taking pictures of sea views on a clear and sunny day from a coastal path between Swanpool and Maenporth, near Falmouth. When he later downloaded the images on to his computer, a round metallic 'craft' was visible in the centre of the shot, about two miles away.

Kelvin was quoted in the *Sun* newspaper as saying:

> There were a couple of tankers out in the bay and I thought that it made a nice shot.
> There was nothing in view and certainly no fault on the camera. When I got home I couldn't believe what I had. I thought, 'Wow where did that come from?' I'm not the sort to believe in UFOs – now I'm not so sure.

Just a week later the *Sun* newspaper was inundated with more pictures and stories of UFO sightings all over the UK. However, what was more interesting was another image of what seems to be a metallic ball-like object floating over a navy ship, which was captured from the very same spot. Other people also came forward to report seeing the 'craft' floating over the horizon.

Another famous sighting recently made the local news, when a number of witnesses reported seeing 'Triangles hovering on the rugged coastline around Tintagel Castle' in two separate incidents. It was reported that 'All but one of the four witnesses refused to be named publicly for fear of ridicule'. The triangle-shaped anomalies were seen on two separate occasions, once on 11 January, just a few hundred yards from Tintagel Castle, and again on 15 February at Polzeath beach, just eight miles away. David Gillham, the Chairman of CUFORG (Cornwall UFO Research Group) was investigating these sightings and was reported to mention that 'Officials at RAF St Mawgan and RNAS Culdrose had been unable to explain the triangle phenomena'. He said, 'We believe something very strange is occurring, and has been occurring possibly for centuries in this part of Cornwall'.

Have aliens landed at Cornish Camelot?

A SPATE of bizarre UFO sightings involving bright geometrical shapes has been reported near Cornish sites linked to the legend of King Arthur.

In two separate incidents witnesses reported white triangles hovering on the rugged coastline around Tintagel Castle, Cornwall – where Arthur was supposedly conceived.

In the third sighting a group of lights formed a square above a lonely moorland road.

The X-Files type mystery involved shapes which appear two-dimensional and move in total silence.

Intriguingly, one witness reported hearing a muffled cry for help seconds before the triangles appeared.

Reports on the sightings, backed by detailed witness state-

BY NICK CONSTABLE

ments, have been logged with the Ministry of Defence by the Cornwall UFO Research Group.

However, the MoD's Secretariat (Air Staff) has refused to investigate further claiming there is 'no evidence that the UK air defence region might have been compromised'.

All but one of the

four witnesses has refused to be named publicly for fear of ridicule.

The first sighting at 6am on January 11 this year occurred a few hundred yards from Tintagel Castle.

A woman was woken by a flashing light in her bedroom.

Through the window the 40-year-old saw a 5ft high triangle flanked by three rows of pulsating red lights.

Dreaming

She went back to bed thinking she was dreaming but returned to the window five minutes later to see two triangles side by side.

The woman, who lives alone, said she was used to seeing tractor lights or the torches of farmers out rabbiting.

She added: 'It wasn't like that. It was extremely bright.'

The second sighting was at 8pm on February 15 at Polzeath beach, eight miles south of Tintagel.

A courting couple walking down to the sea in pitch darkness saw a bright, 20-ft long triangle, flanked by a smaller one, suddenly appear at the top of the beach and float towards the sea.

At one point the shapes were within 12ft of the couple.

They vanished as soon as they touched the waves.

The woman said: 'We heard a noise, I don't know if it was connected.

'It was a cry for help that had just scared me anyway. It was sort of mumbled.

'The triangles didn't hurt my eyes. It became fascinating but it was like, wow, you know. I found myself drawn.

'Then we asked each other: "Did you see that?"'

The third incident occurred in March south of Dozmary Pool, Bodmin Moor – the lake into which Sir Bedivere is said to have hurled Arthur's sword Excalibur.

Drama student Matt Punter, 18, saw a square of lights without substance' hovering eight metres above his car as he drove home late at night.

UFO SPOTTING: Dave Gillham on 'watch' on the beach at Polzeath

All three sightings are expected to be discussed at a conference organised by Cornwall UFO research group at Truro College in September.

Speakers will include the UFOlogist and former BBC sports broadcaster David Icke.

Explain

CUFORG chairman Dave Gillham said officials at RAF St Mawgan and RNAS Culdrose had been unable to explain the triangle phenomena.

He said: 'We believe something very strange is occurring, and has been occurring possibly for centuries, in this part of Cornwall.

'Legend links Tintagel closely with the birth of King Arthur and the magician Merlin. Perhaps there is a hint of truth in some of those legends.'

Reconstruction

lights were here

On 10 October 2009 David Gillham, chairman of CUFORG, was hosting a UFO Conference at Truro College in Cornwall. We managed to catch up with David and ask him a few questions:

'How long have you been interested in ufology and what led you to take an interest?'

Back in 1995 I was sitting in my front room around 9.45 p.m. with the lights off watching a programme on TV; I could see a light in the sky through my dining room. I decided to go into the garden to investigate the light, I soon realised that it was a helicopter travelling from the west to east which is unusual – I live under the helicopter flight path for the Royal Cornwall Hospital and this helicopter was on a different flight path, normally they fly east to west or from south-west to north-east. After watching the helicopter fly down the valley out of sight I turned round to come indoors.

Something red caught my attention. I spun back round to get a better look and I then saw two red lights glowing brightly, floating just above the trees; there was no noise coming from these lights. The lights were side by side moving down the valley, it was just getting dark so I was unable to make out any shape. I went indoors to call my wife out to witness these lights. Her initial thought was that it was a helicopter; I explained that there had been no noise, and they seemed too low. I decided to go out and investigate. I went up to the rear of Richard Lander School, which had good views over the valley and with its elevated position I could look over the whole valley – it was now about 10.05 p.m.

All of a sudden I could hear a helicopter, then another one appeared, then a third, then a forth, they then started to crisscross the valley as if searching for something. They flew around for five minutes or more, then went down the valley in the same direction as the red lights I had seen earlier, at this point I heard a very loud plane noise come over the top of my location, which was very low indeed, which struck me as being very low for this area just outside Truro. I don't know why but I had a feeling that this plane was an RAF Nimrod backing up the helicopters.

The next day I phoned Culdrose control tower to ask why these helicopters were flying so low over the woods at Nansavallan, in reply he explained that he was not on duty, so did not know.

Some months later I received a call; this person explained that he had been entering the petrol station next to the Country Arms, overlooking Nansavallan woods, at about 2 a.m. when he witnessed a very large ball of light hovering just over the power lines. This was when I decided to start Cornwall UFO Research Group.

We went on to ask about how people interested in UFOs could get started on the subject. We were told that Graham Birdshaw, the founder of the 'UFO Magazine', developed a document which is ideal for beginner ufologists. Some pointers from that document are as follows:

1. Pick a secluded spot away from the hustle and bustle of cities, towns and villages and get accustomed to your surroundings. Make a note of natural light, street lights and potential traffic to avoid reporting sightings of everyday occurrences.

2. Use a compass to gather and determine your bearings. Note which objects are to which direction and attempt a guess at their distance. It is best to do this before dark.

3. Night-vision binoculars are a must for any hardcore ufologists; however, these are hard to come by and can be extremely expensive. A standard set of binoculars will do the job but you have to be careful of atmospheric distortion which can be magnified by these tools.

4. Digital cameras and camcorders with infrared are also a handy tool to have and can allow you to look back on potential anomalies and apply certain tests to confirm or deny the captured object.

5. Finally, patience is a major factor in any sky watch.

Other regular reported sightings over Cornwall, and in fact across the UK, are mysterious floating orange lights that seem to drift across the sky. The following are just a few of the stories that can be found on the www.uk-ufo.co.uk website.

A view of Summerleaze beach at Bude.

On 9 September 2009, at 10.50 p.m., two people saw 'around twenty orange lights travelling at speed across the sky from Fowey and disappearing abruptly over Charleston. There was no engine noise and they were not flying in any particular formation'. In response to this report, other sightings of the same orange lights were seen on 12 September between 9.30 p.m. and 11 p.m. in St Austell, all heading in the same direction; they were noticed by three different people.

At 10.15 p.m. on 19 September 2009 at least two people saw 'three bright orange lights in a clear sky at equal distance travelling from north-west to south' while in St Ives.

On the website there are at least another twenty reports from witnesses of strange orange lights floating across the sky and then fading to nothing. Some explain that they pulsate while others say that they move in a certain direction before erratically changing course. Many sceptics believe that these are simply Chinese lanterns that have been released. However, with regards to the reports on 9 and 19 September, the witnesses specifically mention that they are familiar with Chinese lanterns and that what they saw was definitely not these.

The ideal locations for UFO phenomena seem to have been identified and recorded as open, barren land or along the coastline. The shape and content of Cornwall makes it a perfect location for UFO sightings. North Cornwall has experienced its fair share of unusual aerial activity and various crafts have been reported by the media. On one such occasion a UFO was

A view of the Hurlers, with Cheesewring in the background.

tracked from the south coast of Wales and eventually appeared over and around Bude in North Cornwall. This very craft had apparently been followed by the air force and was later reported by residents to the Devon and Cornwall police. Unfortunately, no more information could be gleaned regarding this story.

As well as being home to ancient monuments, unusual stone formations and tales of a beast that roams, Bodmin Moor is also well known as a place for groups to go UFO spotting. On a clear, moonlit night the view from Cheesewring at the top of Minions is absolutely spectacular. Whether or not you are a UFO enthusiast, you are likely to see some unusual light phenomena most evenings in the vast sky arena above you. The lack of light pollution makes this area an amazing place to lie back and look up at the stars. It is worth spending a few hours on a warm summer evening relaxing and watching the sky. When you do see something unusual it makes it all worthwhile. It is unknown what this activity in the sky is; it could be planes, satellites or shooting stars. Then again it could be something else, maybe an alien spacecraft?

Make up your own mind if you will!

Crop Circles

As well as Cornwall being a hot spot for UFO activity, it is also known for its landscape artistry of shapes and intricate designs that have adorned the fields of corn and barley. It is believed that more crop circles have been found in the South West than in any other part of the UK.

An example design of a crop circle found in the many fields around Cornwall.

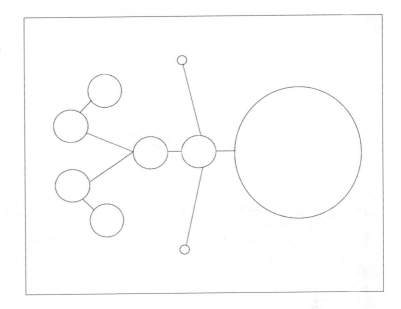

What has become a farmer's nightmare has also become the focus for thousands of people proclaiming that the little green men have been carving into the countryside canvas.

According to the *Falmouth Packet* in June 2008, Helston became the focus of a mysterious design on what was seemingly a normal Sunday evening. A lady who resides near the field where the circle was found was interviewed by the paper and was quoted as describing the phenomenon as 'bent over in a perfect spiral pattern', stating that there were 'outer rings with the corn left standing upright inside them'. RNAS Culdrose and the Crop Circle Organisation were contacted about this phenomenon in the hope that they could get a shot of the design from the sky.

There are many theories about what crop circles are and how they are created. Certain websites describe the exact way to create a hoax design, including step-by-step instructions and a warning to make sure you have permission to start reshaping the field you plan to design in. Other experts, such as Brian Hussey, suggest a range of reasons for how these amazing shapes have come about. Most of his theories relate to natural phenomena such as whirlwinds, vortexes, magnetic and earth related energy. Other theories imply religious connotations, explaining that these shapes usually pop up near sacred sites such as Stonehenge or near churches. Of course, there is also the usual UFO theory that these amazing creations are produced by the visitation of alien spaceships, or are crafted by the alien beings themselves. Evidently there is one theory, believed by the majority of people, that they are hoax designs cleverly thought up, probably by students or farmers, to attract media attention.

Regardless of the reasons for their existence, no one can deny their beauty in design, or their far-reaching appeal which has made them a phenomenon noticed worldwide.

NINE

HAUNTED HOTELS

The former holiday village of Duporth Manor is thought to be haunted by the ghost of Flo the nun, said to be responsible for the sounds of striking matches being heard and many other mysterious events. These have been witnessed by both guests and security staff; the site has now been developed as a new residential area. Only time will tell if Flo has moved on to leave the new residents in peace.

At Perranporth it is said there is (or rather was) a haunted cabin on one of the caravan sites. Being awoken in the night by heavy footsteps outside, two ladies saw the door burst open and then slam shut of its own accord. The footsteps then appeared to be emanating from the lounge; on venturing in they were greeted by the sound of rustling paper and chuckling, along with the empty rocking chair swaying as if someone was sitting in it. The final straw was the sound of a low growl heard from behind this chair in the clearly empty room.

Holiday encounters are not just a modern phenomenon, as far back as the 1850s there is an account of a woman staying at a farmhouse on Looe Island. She experienced the strange blue lights, also witnessed by others, as well as the figure of a tall aristocratic man enveloped in a blue haze who subsequently disappeared through a wall. The story goes that many years later the skeleton of a man with unusually long fingers was discovered.

Towards the end of a largely uneventful investigation carried out on a Cornish holiday park, one of the researchers returned in a shaken state with what he described as a once-in-a-lifetime experience. He had been sitting inside looking out across a courtyard, when he saw two figures moving between the windows opposite. It was confirmed by a locked off camcorder and motion sensor that no one was in this area, and interestingly several cats were observed earlier staring out of the same window.

Long Cross Hotel, Trelights, near Port Issac

Back in the early 2000s a series of investigations were conducted here by the Ghost Club Society, two of which Stuart was invited to attend. Guests and staff had reported many strange encounters from some quite aggressive poltergeist activity in one of the adjoining cottages; also, sightings and strange feelings were experienced within the hotel itself. The hotel takes its name from the stone cross beside the road outside. On approach, the front of the hotel does give off a gothic, almost stereotypical, haunted ambience. While whatever was once in the cottage

The Long Cross Hotel takes its name from an ancient stone cross beside the nearby road.

appeared to have moved on, there was one room in particular which retained an oppressive feel. It was in this room that members of the team experienced strange black shadows darting around, and at one point three people witnessed the outline of a black figure briefly manifest twice along one of the external walls. It would appear that the group was joined by someone else during one of the vigils, as a smoothed-out bed later showed a depression in the covers at the foot end. From a running camcorder it was clear that no one from this world was responsible. However, during the next visit, nothing untoward occurred; was this due to the group's increased familiarity with the building, or because whatever was haunting the Long Cross had moved on? They may have even moved outside, as in 2005 a woman driving on the B3314 towards Tintagel pulled over after believing she may have hit something – what she presumed to be an animal had darted out in front of her. She saw a woman dressed in Victorian clothing staring at her from the middle of the road before vanishing.

Jamaica Inn, Bolventor, near Bodmin

The famous Jamaica Inn is one of Cornwall's best known landmarks, serving as a welcome rest for many travellers over this former coaching inn's 280-year history. One of the oldest stories is of a stranger (some say a sailor) who left his half-finished tankard on the bar after being called outside. The next day his body was found on the moor; his death remaining a mystery, many have since seen his ghost sitting on the wall outside, refusing to acknowledge any attempts at conversation. The road alongside claims its own place in history as the first ever tarmac road.

Room 5 is one of the rooms where many – including Living TV's *Most Haunted* – have reported an eerie experience. The spectre of a woman has been spotted here. Members of the SI team have taken part in three investigations in Room 5; the highlight of the first was a strange

Jamaica Inn. On the road between here and Five Lanes an old-fashioned car, containing four laughing men, was witnessed on at least two occasions during the 1970s before disappearing without trace.

light anomaly caught on camcorder while a psychic was dowsing, best described as being like two balls of light connected by a flexible line or cord. This was captured in the former generator room, just outside of the smaller bar; both areas are home to multiple sightings and encounters. This area is now a second reception and, during the second two visits, even those unaware of the history and previous findings remarked on this area as feeling very uncomfortable. Within Room 4, the most unusual experience happened during the last visit, when coat hangers were heard banging together from within an empty wardrobe. But alas, no sign of the previously reported figure of a man, also seen wandering the inn, or the phantom noises echoing from the courtyard. Two solicitors had their stay interrupted by voices talking in a strange language outside (old Cornish perhaps?); and the sound of cart wheels crunching on gravel; unbeknown to them the courtyard was originally gravel, the cobbles only being laid some twenty-five years earlier.

Camelot Castle, Tintagel

Camelot Castle now serves as a Mecca for artists of all media. The great hall has huge peach marble pillars of Dolomite origins, large tree ferns, splendid works of modern art along with a spectacular round table and a Strad concert piano dating from 1830. Noel Coward is rumoured to have played this very piano and Camelot has also seen many stars of screen and music enjoy a relaxing stay, overlooking one of England's most beautiful coastlines. There is a timeless sensation here, particularly on the upper levels or while enjoying a fine dining experience in the former ballroom, with waiters dressed as if onboard the *Titanic*. Guests of the hotel aren't likely to be disturbed by any paranormal phenomena in the night; in fact, following two lengthy investigations only two adjoining rooms displayed anything out of the ordinary. This included an isolated rap on the window frame, bizarre sensations of static electricity and a loud bang and 'ting' being heard, as if unseen hands had thrown something at a light shade.

In keeping with the previous activity, visual and audio encounters occurred outside the hotel on the headland overlooking the medieval ruins of Tintagel Castle and above Baras Nose, said to have been home to an ancient monastery. On two separate occasions a figure was witnessed

Inside Camelot Castle – originally built as King Arthur's Castle Hotel in 1899 by the Victorian architect Sylvanus Trevail, who was also responsible for the Headland Hotel at Newquay.

The sea-facing side of Camelot, where a spectral figure is seen walking towards Tintagel Castle on the right.

out of the hotel's windows gliding across the artistic stone circle on the headland before disappearing. Another was observed by the service tunnel, an area known to the staff as one not to be alone in. It is believed that this shade is the ghost of a former electrician who lived at the cottage below (opposite the current Tintagel Visitor Centre) making his way home down the precarious single-track path. Definitely not a route to be taking alone on in the middle of the night due to its rough condition and severity of gradient; we can be pretty confident this was not just somebody taking a walk who then vanished in plain view. This cottage, now privately owned, is also said to be haunted by this former employee. A metallic banging sound was heard twice in this same area, the side of the hotel facing Tintagel Head. Likened to a flagpole or heavy fence banging in the wind, there is nothing of the sort here, so the question remains: was this echoes of a phantom skirmish being replayed or simply something mundane being carried in the wind? None of the team has reported anything similar before or since, suggesting at least that the powerful energy many feel along these cliffs is very real.

Headland Hotel, Newquay

Fellow investigators Clare Buckland and Dave Hallybone joined Stuart on a cold, damp, windy night in 2007 for an investigation in this grand hotel, sat on the headland overlooking Newquay's famous Fistral Beach. Two of the hotel's many suites were presented to us as being particularly active, with reports from both guests and staff; several avoided working alone in these two rooms whenever possible. The first of these rooms saw nothing significant take place, the same was true of the second, although at one point an investigator did hear footsteps on the staircase leading up. We opened the door expecting a member of the hotel staff to be joining us but there was no one there, and this set of stairs led only to the one suite, the other rooms being too far away for someone to have double-backed out of sight.

The billiard room has seen several independent reports of a dark figure appearing in three of the four corners of the room; sadly this did not occur despite group and lone vigils being carried out. We did agree that the nearby children's room had a most unusual feel to it, and while moving from here to the cellar area Dave excitedly asked if anyone had brushed past him. He had felt the equipment case in his hands suddenly become lighter as if someone had given him a helping hand. We were later told that this is an area the staff don't like to work alone in due to a multitude of similar experiences and, with the lights all on, it was clear that no one had moved anywhere near to Dave.

Headland's grand reception and restaurant area only offered the one strange event: an isolated cold blast of air across the face. Normally we would be quite sceptical of this sort of report, but the area was completely empty with absolutely no evidence of draughts to be

The Headland Hotel is very exposed, with the energy of the waves surrounding the building – could this offer a possible explanation for reported phenomena?

Headland's grand staircase across from the imposing dining room; perhaps the splendour of the décor creates a formal atmosphere, almost as if you shouldn't be there?

found. It did seem as though the hotel's atmosphere calmed down after 2 a.m., which does seem to fit with the building's previous use as an RAF hospital during both world wars. After all, at this time those unable to sleep would surely have been sedated to ensure rest for the other patients.

Queens Head Hotel, St Austell

St Austell (Sen Ostell in Cornish) was the centre of the china clay trade within Cornwall during the mid-nineteenth and early twentieth centuries. The effects of this are still with us today, as according to the 2001 census St Austell has the largest population of any Cornish town, including the regional capital city of Truro. Dave Hallybone investigated the Queens Head in August 2006 and was left puzzled by a couple of very strange experiences, which he has not experienced before or since. Guests of the hotel will be pleased to know that none of these occurred within any of the bedrooms. Dave recalls how he sometimes felt the building to be confusing, due to its narrow width and the corridors all looking exactly the same. He recalls experiencing a strange lethargic feeling, which almost put him into a trance-like state (most unusual for Dave to report as an experienced and level-headed investigator). This was interrupted by a series of four distinct raps in response to another member of the team calling out to any spirits who might be present. Again this was repeated on request, with a second series of four raps being heard by all present. Several of the team also reported hearing a cat meow while in the bar, despite there being no cat in the hotel. Perhaps any ghosts here are of animals, rather than humans – Dave also reported the feeling of being nuzzled by a dog, despite there clearly being nothing near to him to create such a sensation.

Charlestown used to serve as a busy port to St Austell and is said to have many of its own ghostly goings on. (Picture kindly provided by Darren Rollings)

Land's End Hotel Complex, Land's End, near Sennen

There is a wide variety of hauntings reported from several of the buildings making up this tourist landmark. One we encountered was confined to a particular room in the hotel, which had a most hostile feel to it; this was also felt in the corridor, almost inducing a sense of panic. Sounds were heard coming from this corridor and the adjoining rooms; we were fortunate enough to be able to check these and they were locked and empty, providing no reason for the ghostly whisperings being heard by several people at once.

Some twenty-eight miles over the sea lies the archipelago of the Scilly (or 'fortunate') Isles, St Mary's being home to two more allegedly haunted hotels: England's southernmost hotel, the Bell Rock Hotel and the magnificent Elizabethan Star Castle Hotel dating from 1593. The latter takes its name from the bastion walls angled to provide a network of supportive fire.

Outside of the main complex is a building, now used as a store; many of the staff avoid this area and it is all too easy not to notice it as you drive onto the site. Known as Hallam Vean or the Devil's House, this building is alleged to have been specifically built as a séance hotel during the early twentieth century as the spiritualist movement congregated *en masse* in the Sennen area. It was striking how quiet this building was, hardly a sound was heard – no rattling windows in the wind, no settlement noises – very unusual for an old building in an exposed location and it certainly set the scene very well. After a prank was played by one investigator

Land's End – the most fantastic place to watch stars in the night sky.

jumping out at the others from concealment, the resulting laughter was short-lived, as the motion sensor went off in the hallway, which was separated by two closed doors. This was a phenomenon restricted to this area which also occurred during a second investigation, again while no one was in the area. Later on in the same room, one of us clearly heard the sound of a dog barking outside during a quiet vigil – an unnerving experience as the rest of the team were all much closer to the only window in the room and did not hear a thing! In a room opposite this, four of us heard an unexplainable knock, as if a glass was being rapped on the shelving. The lights were on at the time and the only glass present was clearly visible on a chair between members of the team.

Wellington Hotel, Boscastle

Thomas Hardy is one of the many famed guests to have stayed at the former 'Bos Castle Hotel', renamed and extended after the death of the 'Iron Duke' of Wellington. High above on 'Corkscrew Hill' is another of Boscastle's oldest buildings, the Napoleon Inn, said to have served as a recruiting office during the Napoleonic wars. Some say more for the side of the French due to the profits from the smuggling trade, especially brandy. There is a tale from Mevagissey of a monkey washed ashore from a wrecked French ship during this time; the villagers hanged the poor creature, believing it to be a French spy!

Dating from the sixteenth century and one of Cornwall's most famous haunted hotels, the 'Welly' is also, perhaps, our favourite.

The Wellington Hotel dates from the sixteenth century and, while a glimpse of its ghostly residents is not guaranteed, you will receive a warm welcome from Tamsyn and the staff, as well as enjoying some of the finest cuisine in the area. The dining room exudes a grand feeling of splendour, which after dark takes on a more sinister tone. Well known to several former staff members is the sighting of a man with a ponytail, dressed in a ruffled shirt and leather gaiters; observed as a real person at first, he then disappears through a wall near the reception. The sad shade of a young girl said to have been crossed in love has been seen on many occasions as she drifts forlornly around the hotel, particularly the tower's top landing.

Room 10 is thought by many to be the most active; it is believed to have been used as a mortuary, for storing bodies before they were taken up Coffin Way, the track leading up the side of the valley from the beer garden. A very large piece of slate was found stashed in the attic above Room 10, which can still be seen in its new guise as a picnic table. The only obvious use for such an expensive and perfectly-shaped piece of slate would be as a mortuary slab.

Figures have been seen in the corridor and an old woman was witnessed by a retired police officer, also seen by staff, to enter Room 9, which was unoccupied at the time. A figure was witnessed along the corridor leading here during one of our visits, and the person concerned was visibly shaken by the experience. One of the most interesting events occurred after we had retired for the night, and was heard by four people in two different rooms; the morning was well upon us by this point. From Room 20 our colleague, Clare Buckland, had woken to find her sister Jenny in the bathroom when she heard a series of loud noises, as if someone was running or falling down the stairs from rooms 23 and 22. In Room 21 a similar experience was reported, including what sounded like two girls giggling in the corridor outside. Interestingly, nothing at all was heard from the guests in Room 22 or from Stuart staying in Room 23. But he did have an overwhelming compulsion to check the corridor outside the room before going to sleep, leaving a camcorder running in the room facing the door. Several others felt they were not alone in their rooms, one feeling a sensation of his foot being stood on and another witnessing a dark shadow move from the *en-suite* before passing through the room door. It was only during breakfast, when we discussed our experiences, that we found out

The spiral labyrinth stone carving set at the beginning of Coffin Way, and opposite the slate mortuary-slab table.

guests often hear children playing or running up and down the same flight of stairs.

Following our second visit, with a largely different team, it was interesting to see how the activity was all in the same areas as identified during our first night and by the staff before this. It would appear that one of the former resident ghosts, 'The Waiter', may have disappeared with the floods of 2004, as he failed to make an appearance during either of our investigations. The manager, Suzanne Roberts, related to us the only notable recent guest experience since our investigations of 2005 and 2007:

> She described a presence in the room and a feeling like a rush of cold air, then total paralysis for about thirty seconds, after which she was free to move again and felt 'fine'. The guest described her experience as 'terrifying' and was not best pleased on her departure; however, this is the first time we have heard of anything like this.

We would add to this that the 'Welly' has always felt comfortable and inviting during our visits, never giving a sense of fear – more of fascination of the strange goings-on within.

Kings Arms, Penryn, near Falmouth

The Kings Arms hotel is located in one of the oldest locations in Cornwall, in the small fishing village of Penryn. It is purported to be over 600 years old. On entering this hotel you can see and feel the history it holds. It was reported to be owned by the Edgcumbe family between the seventeenth and nineteenth century, before becoming an inn as it is today.

There are a lot of stories related to the Kings Arms and its murky past. In 1888 a local survey allocated a number to the site, as they did with all buildings in this area. What was interesting was that the number allocated was 666. It is also reported that three separate exorcisms have taken place in the building behind the Kings Arms, all of which apparently failed to remove the malevolent entity that haunts it.

Alleged activity includes: electrical anomalies such as the television turning itself on and off, the sounds of rushing water, and internal doors rattling when no one is around. Also, a little girl has been seen at the end of the bed in one room and a builder has refused to work after dark

The Kings Arms.

after encountering a presence on the landing. Clothes have been found scattered around the room, even though they had previously been folded into drawers. During restoration work the owners discovered a bricked-off stairway leading to the second floor; reasons for this are so far unknown.

The current owners have had their own encounters within the building: while shutting up one night, the landlord felt as though something was moving in the bar area; he decided to follow it through to the back of the building and at this point he felt as though he was being dragged backwards. The landlady, who had followed him, saw a large grey mist behind, in the direction of the recently altered restaurant, which was originally a cobbled courtyard.

Penryn is also home to a legendary coach complete with headless horses, said to appear over the festive period. It is ill-advised to look intently at this spectral carriage, for if the legend is true you will be whisked away to another realm.

The Church of St Gulvias is said to be haunted by a former bell-ringer who later became a ship's captain and drowned at sea. His shade has been encountered silently standing in the church and, on occasion, is said to be responsible for unprompted bell-ringing in the early hours.

TEN

PENGERSICK CASTLE AND PARANORMAL RESEARCH

Surrounded by landscaped gardens and woods, partly restored to a medieval appearance, there is an air of magic to Pengersick Castle, described by those who live and work here as 'where the veil between this world and the next seems permanently thin'. A subject of our ongoing research, Pengersick's tower comprises four storeys, each with a single room off the sixty-five-step granite spiral staircase, and an open-roof level. From up here the castle's proximity to Praa Sands beach comes as a surprise, given the castle's sweeping woods which surround it on two sides. The tower was constructed for the dual purpose of residential use and refuge, from the very real threat of French or Spanish marauders and Barbary pirates.

Pengersick is derived from the Cornish for 'head of a marshy place' or 'silted up inlet'; the stream which still runs past it to the sea provides evidence that its name was once appropriate.

The grounds as seen from the tower roof, as they were ten years ago before restoration.

The current tower is built from stone reclaimed from an earlier house, the site of which is in the castle's grounds, and it is from here that many of Pengersick's spectral inhabitants originate. As a manor it dates back to at least 1199, and over the years the ambition of its owners has seen the estate grow, partly through calculated marriages to improve their status. Heirs of the Pengersick inheritance have held such celebrated positions as Governor of St Michael's Mount.

Ghostly monks have been witnessed within the grounds of Pengersick, and a suggested reason for their appearance is one of its former occupants, Henry Le Fort. The 'lawless Pengersick' was excommunicated in 1330 for an attack on the vicar of Breage, who was visiting with a monk from Hailes Abbey, Gloucestershire, to collect tithes. The other of Pengersick's most infamous owners, John Milliton from Meavy, Devon, married into the family in 1470. It is he (along with Henry Le Fort, according to some sources) who is alleged to have practised the black arts of witchcraft and sorcery. Some believe this to be the origin of much of the activity reported at Pengersick, but it is likely that such stories were encouraged to keep away suspicious neighbours, the Church, and of course, the law. John, the son of John Milliton, was accused of illegally acquiring many treasures from the wreck of the Portuguese carrack flagship, *St Anthony*. It is from this notorious period in the family's history that the rumours of tunnels leading down to the nearby beach originate. There is some evidence of this, as the castle often has salt water coming through the floor in the gun room.

The late owner, Angela Evans, puts it very concisely in her own words:

> There are those who recall tales of the old days when Pengersick had a reputation for black magic, sorcery and all kinds of wickedness — a place to be avoided after dark. What better refuge could there be for the spoils of wreckers and smugglers?

Praa Sands, less than half a mile away from the castle. This stretch of coast had the reputation of being the worst in Cornwall for wreckers and their savage behaviour.

The gun room still appropriately contains arms and armour, along with an illustration of how the castle would have originally looked as a fortified manor.

Angela would seldom talk of her own experiences within the tower, but we know that she was not sceptical.

No matter what you believe about ghosts and the spirit world, Pengersick is one of those places which has an effect on people. If nothing else, there is at least a sense of enchantment about this place which takes over you. During the course of vigils held at Pengersick Castle over the last twelve years, we have encountered many unusual events. While some visits have been less than eventful, by and large something new and inexplicable has occurred with each visit. The following is an account of perhaps our most active and enlightening visit towards the end of 2008. It does focus on activity experienced in the bedroom, and summarises much of the sensations experienced by investigators and visitors to the castle over many years; it would, however, take the whole of this book to detail all the paranormal events experienced.

We were not using any equipment, only waiting to observe phenomena, rather than the more usual practice of trying to interact with any spirits present using dowsing and other psychic methods. The atmosphere in this room does seem to change from neutral to … as if something really quite strong is building at times. One investigator reported the sensation of being touched and of nausea, another member of the team saw a green circle of light briefly appear to the right-hand side of her forehead. It was so severe that she had to leave the room and was clearly not herself for some time after – most unusual behaviour for her, not repeated before or since. Blasts of cold air were felt by the team in the bedroom and within the solar room below. Often these were experienced on demand and, to reassure the sceptics, we are

Looking through the eighteenth-century four-poster bed into the spiral staircase beyond – which of course turns to the right, so the defender's sword arm was free to swing down on any intruders climbing the tower steps.

Pengersick's haunted bedroom. Regular ghost nights are run here by Rita Ratcliffe-Marshall and the Cornwall Paranormal Organisation; bookings can be made by contacting info@CPOonline.co.uk

quite used by now to ruling out natural drafts and normal temperature variations. Humidity levels were around seventy per cent – too high to account for the effect of low humidity drying out skin and creating the sensation of being touched. The sensations of nausea and being prodded are common here as is the feeling of being watched, often most unwelcoming. Also reported, and on this occasion by two investigators at the same time, are visual encounters.

Two experienced and trusted researchers both reported a 'smoky shape' above the chest at the end of the bed, at the same time from two different angles. Another reported what she described as a dark mass spreading across the floor in more or less the same area. This instantly reminded Stuart of the findings from the studies carried out here in 2000 and 2003. No one in Supernatural Investigations was aware of the dark mass of smoke previously reported as emanating from the fireplace and moving along the foot of the bed. Indeed many, including dowsers and psychics, have dismissed these previous findings, as the mist is referred to as a demonic dog. Nor was any of the team aware of the 'wisp' caught on video camera here in 2003 by Anthony Simms (this impressive footage can be viewed on our website and is the best example of unexplainable footage we have captured in twelve years of research); again this appears just in front of the chest. Other shadows were reported which again fit in with past experiences; sadly there was no sign of the spectral figure witnessed outside by two very sceptical team members back in 2003. At first this was presumed to be one of the team, but on approach the figure with its 'wispy, flowing hair' was nowhere to be seen and everyone was accounted for, still inside the bedroom.

Not too far from Pengersick Castle is the historical Godolphin House and Godolphin Cross. The house is said to be home to a White Lady, which many associate with Lady Margaret, the wife of the first earl, Sydney Godolphin. Her legendary beauty was cut short in her mid twenties when she died during childbirth. She is said to appear on the anniversary of her death, 9 September 1678. Peter Underwood describes her as originating from a long-sealed closet in the entrance hall, moving out to the terrace then through an avenue of old trees walking 'discontentedly among the shadows'. Godolphin House allegedly contains five escape routes, built to aid King Charles II, which can only add to the building's sense of mystery. Those sleeping in the guest room, including the historian Dr A.L. Rowse, have reported 'the unmistakable swish of a lady's silk dress'. Anthony Hippisley Coxe describes how nearby Jew Lane is haunted by the ghost of a Jew who committed suicide by hanging himself from a tree and whose resting place is said to be beneath the road. It was standard practice, until relatively recent times, to bury suicides in unconsecrated ground, often at crossroads, so that they could not find their way home to visit the living. Slightly less feasible is the account that the ghost takes the form of a bull and fiery chariot.

The professional dowsers Alan Neal and Ron Kirby, along with their colleagues, have spent considerable time conducting an archaeological study of Pengersick Castle and its grounds. As well as mapping the outline of the old manor house, they have led the owners to new finds, later confirmed by geophysical surveys. Ron summarises on his website a dowser's perspective of the paranormal, one remarkably similar to our own:

> There is much debate as to exactly what paranormal phenomena are, and even as to whether such things even exist outside the imagination of some rather hysterical or susceptible people.
> If, as seems likely, strong thought forms can in some way become attached to buildings, this may

The Merry Maidens stone circle at Boleigh. Legend tells of how nineteen maidens danced to the tune of two pipers — they were all turned to stone for making merry on the Sabbath.

be an explanation for ghosts and other apparitions. Because thoughts are 'living' things and are capable of being used, it is possible that traumatic events even generate such intense emotions in a person that the energy vibration of these thoughts and feelings become imprinted in some way on the buildings and remain there long after the person's physical death. In certain circumstances these thought forms may become re-enacted so that 'ghosts' appear.

The late archaeologist Thomas Charles Lethbridge was probably the first scientist to use the ancient art of dowsing for detecting paranormal entities. Besides this and its more common application for finding water and mineral ore, dowsing can be used to trace both earth energy and ley lines. Alan Neal differentiates between the two by defining the first as being of natural origin, similar to the concept of Ch'I, and the second as being man-made examples of 'Completely straight alignment across the landscape of places of historic and prehistoric importance.'

While we can only touch on the vast subject of energy and ley lines here, it is clear that a large number of sites with paranormal associations are on, or close to, such alignments. Many UFO sightings have been reported in their vicinity, while the Cardinham area, prowling ground for Big Cats, is by the St Martin ley.

Duloe stone circle also sits on this line, while the Hurlers of St Cleer on Bodmin Moor are on the St Michael line. Of course, exactly why such circles were constructed is something of an enigma. In explaining their purpose our ancestors used a religious moral: the Hurlers were said to be men turned to stone for the sin of playing on the Sabbath, while the Nine Maidens near St Columb Major are said to be the spirits of nine maidens, with a fiddler at their centre, frozen forever for the same crime.

King Doniert's Stone (right), pictured here with the 'Other Half Stone', is believed to have been erected for the last recorded Cornish king.

The Hurlers is an ancient collection of upright stones said to possess a positive energy.

The Prayer Tree, where the majority of visitors to Madron find serenity and remembrance.

Bodmin Moor is also home to two large stones, sited between Golitha Falls and Siblyback Lake. King Doniert's Stone is said to name the last recorded Cornish king; it is believed that the stone was erected after his death. The fellow medieval stone is known as the 'Other Half Stone' and sits alongside King Doniert's Stone. Both stones may have been medieval crosses and it does seem as though the pieces that are left are simply a portion of what existed originally.

Not just stone circles, but also cairns, quoits and holy wells are found along both earth and ley energy lines. Just outside the village of Madron are two wells; the only one still fully accessible is set in the corner of a ruined chapel. On approach is a colourfully decorated tree, known as the 'Prayer Tree', said by many to share some of the healing waters associated with the site. A custom still very much alive today is the tying of small pieces of cloth, and other trinkets, to the tree, along with messages – all thought to bring health to the sick and to help remember the dead. The well at Ludgvan is reported to have cured sore eyes; it is also said that any child baptised here could never be hanged with a hempen rope. St Ruth (and his red cloak) lends his name to a well near Redruth, another said to prevent any child baptised there from being hanged. St Non's Well at Hobb's Park Farm, Pelynt, is known as 'Piskie's Well', and it is said the pixies can be prevented from mischief by gifts of pins. Altarnun, further north, is home to a well devoted to St Non; it is said to have been used in the cure of lunacy. The holy well in the village of Roche is said to have divinatory properties, often lunatics or 'frantic persons' were immersed in the well as a means of curing them by driving out their unholy demons.

The well at St Cleer is said to have been used for this purpose, as a 'bowser' or ducking well. Perhaps our favourite holy well is St Keyne's, the waters of which are said to hold the key to mastery in marriage. Newlywed couples would customarily race to the well to see who could be the first to drink, following their exchange of vows. Scarlet's Well in Bodmin is so named because of the curiously coloured waters said to be a good general cure for disease. Liskeard is home to two wells, including 'Pipe Well' – which is said to still have curative properties. Originally named St Martin's Well it had a lucky stone on which engaged couples would drink to ensure fertility.

So far we have focused on the details of paranormal encounters, but have yet to discuss issues such as the current methodologies utilised by paranormal investigators and the application of a scientific analysis.

The chapel well at Madron. Shadowy figures have been encountered in the area leading to it.

'Pipe Well' in Liskeard.

Retrospective analysis of cases and experiences is an often overlooked aspect of the supernatural world, and can lead to explaining some ghostly or otherworldly encounters. Paranormal Site Investigators carried out a detailed investigation into Bodmin Jail during April 2005. Their lead investigator and respected researcher, Dave Wood, reflects on a previously published account featured in Jason Karl's *21st Century Ghosts*, which also featured Pengersick Castle:

Nearly five years on I recognise this as one of our most noteworthy investigations. With over one hundred investigations I have personally attended, to date, most seem to merge into one another; Bodmin Gaol is a notable exception. Although a number of anomalous events appeared to take place on that day, two stick in the mind. The first was a case of hysteria in the naval gaol and the second apparent stone throwing in the middle gaol. In the naval gaol the 'context' of the situation was somewhat 'spooky'. The observer stands at the base of a honeycomb-looking, several storey high gaol, and the cell doors towering above the observer in a disorientating fashion. Former members of the PSI team were overcome by the atmosphere and by an apparent apparition witnessed by two of them. Hysteria is not exactly unheard of in paranormal investigations generally. At the time my assessment was that such hysteria was unprecedented in PSI and has not happened since, but looking back the team were not so experienced or rational at the time. An apparent apparition seen by two people simultaneously is always interesting although it strikes me, now, that as each were reporting simultaneously (almost jointly) that one would have had influence on the other. Subsequent occurrences where two people report seeing an apparition at one time, where the percipients are separated, their testimony is typically very different from one another. The second noteworthy event was several instances of stone throwing on the middle floor. This form of event is not unprecedented and I have experienced a consistent level of stone throwing at another location in nearby Devon. On an instinctive level I would rule out hoax if for no other reason than that several video cameras (including a BBC TV camera) were trained on the team. While the stones were captured on camera the source of the trajectory was not, unfortunately, meaning that the stone throwing of Bodmin Gaol can remain nothing more than an anecdote.

The issue of hysteria affecting a group of people in an eerie context, which most paranormal investigations will undoubtedly be, has been explored by parapsychologists as the preferred explanation offered by the field of psychology. People in such environments are primed to expect paranormal activity, and therefore will report it. The sceptic argument builds on this to provide a general explanation for the majority of reported supernatural encounters. The simple truth is that it's nearly impossible to recreate paranormal events in a controlled laboratory environment to settle the discussion once and for all. This is partly due to the unpredictable and often apparently random nature of such experiences, but also because science has not confirmed the exact factors responsible – is it the location, the time and date, the persons present or something else we have yet to realise?

Dave Wood has also compiled what he terms as 'A New Method of Investigation', following an unprecedented thorough analysis of several years of active investigations. We cannot

Bodmin Jail has seen both our group and PSI experience poltergeist-like phenomena, including stones being thrown in both the civil and naval wings. One investigator experienced the sensation of a small hand grabbing his own – we were unaware that this has often been reported.

recommend enough that all investigators of the supernatural read this radical academic text, which suggests that the paranormal community need to concentrate their efforts, chiefly to present results in a cohesive manner, using a standardised format to allow meaningful comparison, and to separate dubious pseudo-scientific 'evidence' from events that are genuinely unexplainable. Nicky Sewell and the rest of the PSI team have dedicated an entire website to the conclusions of their methodical approach to answering the question of 'orbs', and whether they are of paranormal origin or due to technical flaws misinterpreted by assumption-led approaches fitting into people's faiths or beliefs. We then asked Dave what does ASSAP believe is the single biggest obstacle to obtaining evidence of the paranormal today?

> There are two major barriers to obtaining evidence for paranormal phenomena. The first is demonstrating that an event is unexplained in the first place, and the second is demonstrating that something unexplained is actually paranormal. Almost everyone's efforts are fully focussed on the first of these barriers – most would not believe the second was a barrier at all and we are still no closer to breaking down either barrier. Recording unexplainable events is notoriously difficult. Lab-based experiments involving extra-sensory perception (ESP) and psychokinesis (PK) have proved inconclusive, which leaves little hope for looking for anomalies in controlled fieldwork environments. It should be a huge boost for any hope for 'proof' that for every professional parapsychologist at UK universities, there are literally hundreds of lay investigators and researchers. Our only chance of capturing verifiable evidence is to adopt a method that studies and systematically tracks all xenonormal (unfamiliar but explainable) factors in an environment. Regretfully, such an approach is too costly and time-consuming for most groups, so little progress is being made. The second barrier is one of trying to understand the systems that can explain events that are unexplainable by normal scientific methods, and accepting that just because something is unexplained this is not evidence for it being paranormal.

Supernatural Investigations are interested in ESP testing and in how believers and non-believers uniquely respond to alleged paranormal phenomena. Francesca and Damian Haydon sought permission to utilise Michael Thalbourne's Australian Sheep-Goat scale in our own research about ESP ability and how it is affected by the individual's level of belief in the paranormal. Thalbourne's theory suggests that believers in the paranormal (Sheep) perform better at ESP tests than non-believers (Goats), and that Goats actively avoid hits in order to prove their theory of non-belief. This confirmation bias can lead to Goats scoring below average in ESP tests. Our small sample preliminary study included a good spread of Sheep and Goats and confirms, generally speaking, the hypothesis that participants with a higher score on the Sheep-Goat scale (or Sheep) are more likely to generate hits during ESP testing. Furthermore, we observed that Sheep generally report more paranormal phenomena than Goats during paranormal investigations. We plan to continue our research to test these fascinating theories.

However, the psychology-based answers cannot account for all the mysterious encounters reported, so we would like to leave the reader with some final questions. Do entities such as ghosts retain their living intelligence and the ability to pick and choose when (and to whom) they make an appearance? This could also apply to creatures of legend such as mermaids, alien life forms and sightings of Big Cats. Or is the ultimate reason for such experiences simply a matter of being in the right place at the right time?